Georgia Haven

A LOVE STORY ACROSS STATES AND TIME

MAÍRA RAYANNE

Non-Chronological Order

This memoir is written in a non-chronological format.
Front Cover Photograph: July 2016 - Melbourne, FL

**

Any inquiries should be directed to mairarayanne@yahoo.com
Author: Maíra Rayanne
Category: Non-Fiction, Memoir
Published by BookBaby
ISBN: 978-1-54392-578-4

Editors: Patrick Anderson & Linda Sexton
Book Design: Manuela Moncayo

Dedication

For D.B. –
Thank you for changing me.
To the moon and back.

And to my father, Jose Marcos –
You were the first person to ever believe in me.
This memoir is for you.

Author's Note

Declan knew about the conception of this memoir before I was even sure I wanted to write it myself. From the initial pages of the first draft, he was involved in the parts of the book process that he so choose. Even the name Declan – which means a man of prayer or full of goodness – was his choosing. With that said, while not all names herein are fictitious, Declan's real name, in fact, is omitted from these pages.

Part of honoring and respecting our love story was to establish a level of anonymity, as well as to protect his identity and that of his family, including his daughter. Even though I had his blessing to share a range of intimate details and revelations, some things are still meant to be *ours,* and ours alone.

Contents

PART I –

The Beginnings of Summer

*"And so with the sunshine and the great
bursts of leaves growing on the trees,
just as things grow in fast movies, I had
that familiar conviction that life was
beginning over again with the summer."*

— F. Scott Fitzgerald

1

4th of July

He looked the same yet he was changed, in every way a man can be changed.

As I came around the corner of the second-floor parking lot at the Atlanta-Hartsfield International Airport, with my carry-on luggage chugging along behind me and my cell phone alarm sounding off that it was inching toward midnight, Declan was there, waiting for me. His lips curled into a smile I had not seen in two years. His smile, just as endearing as I remembered it; and the soft lines around his dark brown eyes captured the signs of a man who endured more than what he would have liked. He was a little older now, on the verge of his early forties. I was ten years shy of reaching the same.

"Hey! You made it!" he waved, moving closer to me once I came around in full view getting off the elevator.

It had been two years. Two years since the last time Declan visited me in Miami, and I distressingly dropped him off at the airport, not realizing a lifetime of events would intersect between us before our eyes locked again. Two years since my tears whittled to invisible stains on my face, and months of deafening silence then became the remnants of what our friendship could now barely hold onto.

"Let me help you with that," he offered, taking off my carry-on from over my shoulders. I was only planning to stay in Georgia for 24 hours. It was the day before, upon wrapping up a 4th of July weekend outing with fellow co-workers at a local park in Sunrise, Florida, when I got his randomly peculiar text at home:

"Maíra, I appreciate all you have done for me during this whole mess, I really don't know how I would have made it this far. Just know that I love you."

It was perhaps the second or third time Declan had ever said "I love you" to me in the two years I knew him, as friends typically or maybe not so typically do. But it was only the text message he sent right after that confirmed something was terribly wrong.

He did what?!

In a state of panic, I hopped on the first flight out of Fort Lauderdale, the closest airport to my apartment in the city of Plantation.

"How was your trip?"

"Oh, not bad," I responded, still awestruck that we were standing face to face again after so long. Declan was still just as *handsome,* if not more. "The flight was short, thankfully. Just over an hour so not bad. I considered driving down to the Miami airport, 40 minutes away from me, and hopping on a plane there but the only available flight left the next day. And I wanted to make sure I made it here to Georgia tonight. "

"You really didn't have to go through all this, but I'm not gonna lie, it's good to see you again. And I hope you don't mind me saying so – but your green eyes still look as beautiful and hypnotizing as I remembered them," he said smiling, as he wrapped his arms around my slightly tensed-up back and gave me a tight squeeze. I had almost forgotten how good it was to feel his broad shoulders around me, his almost-six-feet-tall, muscular physique pulling little short me in to his safe cocoon.

"It's really good to see you too."

I waited patiently as Declan grabbed my luggage and hopped it onto a tidied-up space on the back trunk of his old BMW. I could tell he cleaned up his car and made space just for my visit, even though a protein bar wrapper still hung from a small compartment inside the trunk where an extra tire lay underneath.

The wrinkles around Declan's dark eyes appeared more prominent and a little deeper now, yet he had still somehow managed to age so gracefully. His chestnut brown hair looked every bit luscious and full, the kind that simply made me envious of the fact that a man a decade older could possibly have better hair than me. And there was his smile. There was no way around that smile that made you never want to leave its presence. It was as comforting now as it was then.

Not a single sound outside could be heard as we arrived to Declan's five-bedroom house that appeared too big for one person alone. The crackling reverberations of 4th of July fireworks from the night before now lingered in the faded distance. We were forty minutes northwest of Atlanta, in the suburbs of Kennesaw where Declan lived, just enough to get away from all the city noise. I had not been here before. It was my first time at the house that I would soon come to view as both a blessing and a curse.

Time ticked away. In just 24 hours I'd be returning home, but I knew so much needed to be said first. So much that had been left unsaid since I received Declan's second unsettling text, which was ultimately what sent me dashing to the airport:

"I need to tell you something," it read. "And please don't get mad. But I just tried to take my life by turning on the engine inside my car. The thought of my daughter ultimately stopped me."

Hours before, I had collapsed on to the hardwood floors of my messy living room as soon as that second text message pinged on my cell phone screen. I could feel myself start to hyperventilate. I was consumed with worry and dread but I had to project onto Declan an image of calmness. Still, I thought, how could this happen? How didn't I know? I knew Declan was in pain, but I didn't know this much. So I did all I could do in those brief moments before heading off to the airport to see him in Georgia. I got on my knees and prayed.

Lord, you have to help me. Help me help him. Use me as your vessel. Let the Holy Spirit come over me and speak through me. I won't be the one to kick him when he's down. I won't let him feel alone. No. Not as long as he's with me.

Walking into Declan's spacious 3,000-square-foot home for the first time made you feel like you were twirling your way into the lap of luxury. Not too far from one of the main streets in Kennesaw known as Barrett Knoll Parkway, Declan bought this five-bedroom, three-bathroom house just a couple of months after we went our separate ways two years prior, when we first met.

Made up of a large open floor plan and a gigantic, overgrown backyard, perfect for his daughter Bella's trampoline, it was bigger than anything I could have imagined. And it was also pretty empty and bare – three of the five bedrooms were seriously in need of a single piece of furniture. Just a simple loveseat, for example, would do.

There was still so much I wanted to say to Declan even as I situated myself in the hallway and wondered where I should put down my luggage. I needed to provide any bit of hope that would reassure him everything was going to be okay. But it was getting late. And Declan was the type to slip under his thousand-something-count covers, turn on his brown noise app and be fast asleep by the time most kids were only starting to get ready for bed.

Our conversation would have to wait.

"Let me take you upstairs so you can put your stuff down. This is Bella's room," noted Declan.

I had never seen his daughter's room before, not even two years ago when he still lived in the old house, modeled in a similar fashion to this one, just a few miles away. I only stayed in his room then that one time I visited.

The soft and pastel-colored décor on her walls spoke of the blossoming elegance of a young girl about to soon enter her teenage years. Bella's personalized name on the bedroom pillow drew you in with its meticulous cursive handwriting. And a number of stuffed animals, with both teddy bears and penguins alike, sat up straight, propped up neatly next to her bed. This was the room of a father's pride and joy.

I could have stayed up for hours. I wanted to know more about what prompted Declan's text and how he felt about this abrupt reunion of ours. The questions fermenting inside my head gradually increased the more I thought about them.

What had gotten him to this breaking point? Did he need to let out a good cry? Should I hold him in my arms? Did anybody know? Was I the only one he told? What about his faith? Where was God in all of this? What about his daughter? What was he thinking seeing me again after so many years? Did it feel awkward and strange to him? Were we in the same place? Did he feel those butterflies when he saw me too? Was I losing my mind? Was he losing his mind?

"Is there anything you need me to get you?" he asked, his words suddenly interrupting my train of thought. My neurotic nature to overanalyze was getting the best of me, and it hadn't even been an hour since I landed.

"I didn't bring contacts solution. Hmm. Do you have any I could borrow?"

"Sure thing. I'll be right back."

I pretended to sort my things as I waited, careful not to accidentally brush my elbow on any of Bella's belongings and send anything to a crashing thud on her pristine-looking bedroom floor.

Declan suddenly reappeared from the upstairs hallway and placed the contacts solution in my hand, "Here you go. Anything else you need?"

"No, I'm good, thanks." I was still a bit guarded and shy.

"Alright. I'll let you get to sleep then. I know it's past midnight and I'm sure we're both pretty beat," he said, as he gently rubbed his eyes, signaling he, too, was ready for bed. "Thanks again for coming. I'm really glad you came, Maíra. I hope you know I mean that."

I nodded then slightly shifted my body towards his daughter's room when I saw his face lean in, and in a split second I could feel his lips almost touching mine. Without a second thought, and almost impulsively, I turned away.

Did he just try to kiss me? I could have sworn he just tried to kiss me on the lips. Dammit. I wanted to kiss him too. Dammit. I'm a fucking fool! Maybe it was just my imagination? No, no. He definitely tried to kiss me. But why?

Embarrassed as I was, I played it off and said my goodnight, as Declan disappeared into the shadows of his master bedroom and I was left to make sense of what I could have sworn almost just happened.

I would see Declan in the morning. I would listen to the details of everything that transpired in his life these past two months. Every detail that led up to this now 4th of July Monday where, for some reason, he thought the best solution was, in fact, the worst thing he could pin his mind to. I would listen without judgment and be there, once more, as a friend.

A friend who, from the moment she laid eyes on him again at the Atlanta airport, was right back to a place where her feelings never left her.

But I couldn't dare ever tell him. Not like this. Not right now.

2

Cinco de Mayo

A couple of months before I hopped on that plane to Georgia, I entertained the idea of casually dating for the sake of casually dating, and William just so happened to be the one I spent several nights fooling around with in the backseat of my car or on my memory foam bed that no longer had a firm cushioned-layer intact.

A New York native who now called Florida his home, William was as funny as he was kind, adventurous as he was thoughtful – but eventually it became clear that our silly little fling that had lasted for a couple of months was quickly reaching a dead end. We were both a distraction of sorts to each other that was starting to get old. Unspoken *friends with benefits* you could say, though *shameless booty call* would have been more appropriate.

Cinco de Mayo was the one day that gave everybody the perfect excuse to get loud and obnoxiously, I-don't-give-a-fuck drunk throughout various parts of South Florida. Given his Hispanic-Colombian background, I knew William was out with his buddies that night at a bar only 20 minutes away from my place off Broward Boulevard, looking clean cut with one of his gelled-up dark curls hanging on the side of his forehead, and ready to down so many *Jose Cuervo* tequila shots and margaritas, even a rumbustious mariachi band would have tried to intervene.

Just a few years younger than me, in his mid-twenties, he was still living that post-college-not-going-to-slow-down-anytime-soon phase. And in a couple of hours, as it had been the case a number of times before, William would call and ask if he could come over.

Declan was no longer on my mind. It had been almost two years since he broke my heart in Miami, and five months since he last emailed me in mid-December, with his typical let's-catch-up-every-few-months or so chatter. Five months since I shared with him the working title of a book I put on the backburner, to which he enthusiastically referred to the title as a *fucking awesome title.* Five months since he said he would catch up with me soon — again — then never actually did. I was done. I was done holding onto a man who seemed to come around only when convenient.

So I deleted his phone number from my cell phone, determined to never hear or speak to him again — this time for good. I accepted that whatever we had almost two years ago, when we first met, was now buried in the past, six feet in deep and to never be seen again. It was time to really move on and forget about him, as I had done with every other guy before him. But I couldn't.

Something kept holding me back. The truth was, Declan wasn't just "every other guy before him." No matter how many times I made my acquaintance with new romantic prospects, there was a lingering kind of emptiness that nibbled on my ear in the middle of the night, reminding me of all the tenderness and sweet words he once crooned me with. I couldn't shake this emptiness away even if I tried. Not even with William around.

"I'm leaving this place now. Can I come by?"

In a matter of minutes William appeared at my doorstep. Lit up like a kid who beams over the toys he got for Christmas, and where endless drinks and shouts of *"Viva Mexico!"* still pulsated on the confetti-covered walls of the Miami Lakes bar he spent the night going to town with.

I motioned for William to come inside, hoping he wouldn't pay attention to the state of disarray my quaint little apartment was in or how I didn't have time to hop into the shower and quickly wash the built-up oil in my hair. I had just moved to my one-bedroom, cozy nesting place in Broward County, in the heart of Plantation, earlier in the year. But I was still commuting to my three-year job as Managing Editor for a digital publishing company in Miami, in the artsy-hipster neighborhood of Wynwood. But aside from work, there was no other reason for me to stay in the city that drained the life out of me.

I no longer felt like I fit in with the 305 crowd that only cared about how many times they could be rude and obnoxious to people in one day. Living in Broward County now, 40 minutes north of Miami, my everyday work commute suddenly tripled in time, but once 4 p.m. rolled around, I didn't waste a second to climb inside my car and drive to my new place I loved to call home.

While most women would make sure their homes looked its very best for a guest, William's last-minute visit had me rushing to throw scattered laundry clothes into my neglected, run-down closet and then quickly toss sushi dinner leftovers into the back of my fridge. But William didn't seem to notice, as he grabbed my face to kiss me the moment he saw me. Even remaining completely oblivious to my little dog popping a squat right behind him, as Lumee lifted his leg for all to see.

Fluffing up a couple of cushions on my clearly out-of-style, thrift store-bought sofa, I sat down next to William, while he did the honors of pouring us a glass of red wine from a bottle I reserved only for special occasions. Even as there was nothing to celebrate here.

In the background, a black-and-white show rerun of "The Beverly Hillbillies" aired on a random TV channel I just so happened to have it turned on to. "Why is it that every time I come over, you always have your TV on some black and white stuff?" he teased, pressing his lips again against mine.

"I don't know…" I shrugged, kissing him once more. "Guess I'm an old soul of sorts?" Anxious to change the topic, I tapped his knee and cozied up closer to him.

"How was your night?" I asked. "Did you have fun at the bar? Were there a lot of people there?" William knew I was one to ask a million questions when nervous or feeling shy.

"It was great, but it was only missing you, of course."

I could always count on William to be your typical sweet-talking charmer in all the *dale-que-tu-puede* South Florida land.

As we started to get in the heavy throes of our usual passionate make-out sessions, I reminded him that this time my bedroom was off limits. Any lust-filled night between us was now off limits. Except this one. Just this one more time. Because every girl needs that *one more time.*

It wasn't long before I started to pick up the bad habit of comparing every man I met to Declan. Although two years had passed since we casually dated, there was one thing I still longed for. That one thing a woman can never put past her or forget: the sweeping chemistry you feel with another, who can just look at you and without a word, your eyes speak a language of having known each other lifetimes ago. It was the chemistry I tried to picture would exist with any other man since, only to be sorely disappointed every time a guy tried to charm me with his unnatural wit and clear attempt in trying too hard. Because he didn't get *it*. And he didn't have *it*. Whatever *it* was.

"Let's go to my room," I called out to William, finally giving in to my hormones taking center stage. With an empty bottle of wine on my nightstand, I soon found myself sprawled out on my queen bed, seeing imaginary stars on my ceiling and coming undone with puddles of sweat trickling down my chest. Here, chemistry found its resting place in between my thighs and I had no problem with it staying there for the night.

The following morning, before sunlight blasted its way through my freshly-painted, white-framed bedroom window, William collected his clothes and gave me a kiss on the cheek, as I walked with him to my front door to say goodbye. "I'll talk to you later," I muttered under my teeth, knowing it was a flat-out lie. He nodded, and then waved at me as he walked down the hallway.

"You have a good day. Te quiero, boba."

"Te quiero too, tonto," I replied.

Smack in the middle of the lobby floor, my apartment was one to easily attract nosy neighbors who had nothing else better to do than pry into the lives of others who, well, actually had lives. But as I saw William approach the lobby front door, I hoped nobody would catch a glimpse of him leaving my place, or my hair still in a thousand knots from all the rounds of rockin' the bed hard the previous night.

Once William was out of sight and out in the parking lot, I closed my apartment door behind him and behind our sex rendezvous one last time. It was fun while it lasted, I thought, but there was no point in continuing nights of short-lived fun that led to nowhere. William knew it, and I knew it. I'm not crazy about him, anyway, I told myself.

One of my favorite places in Plantation consists of a Starbucks right across the street from my apartment, in a plaza where Publix meets Super Cuts, and a Hallmark Gift Shop seems to be hanging on to dear (retail) life. It was standard routine for me to spend many Friday afternoons here, ordering my usual steaming-hot latte (with coconut milk, please) and ignoring the world around me.

After William started driving back home, I was happy to find my typical *spot* available for me when I arrived. My spot, which was basically nothing more than a worn-out armchair on the farthest right side of the café, felt unusually warm to the touch. The sunlight peered in through the glass window next to it, making it unnecessary for the employees to flip on any light switch and add on to their already high electricity bill. People were in line ordering whatever they needed for that afternoon rush to get through the final hours of the day, and I sat down in my *spot* with my laptop open for a little bit of rest and relaxation. It was time to catch up on the latest celebrity gossip news.

I zoned out reading about a recently engaged Hollywood couple when my cell phone started to vibrate and a *new text message* notification came in.

No name appeared (apparently I didn't have this person saved in my Contacts List), but I recognized the not-so-random numbers immediately.

"Hey there. Long time no speak. I know I haven't reached out to you and never even responded to your email in December. I'm so sorry for disappearing. You have every reason to be upset at me and I will understand if you don't respond. I've just been going through a lot of personal issues. It's not an excuse, it's just the truth. Anyway. How are you?"

It was Declan. Five months had rolled by without a peep from him yet here he was again, now in May. *Look what the cat dragged in.*

("He just contacted me. Apparently he's going through some stuff," I texted my best friend, Oceana. "Geez, aren't you glad you dodged that bullet?" she sighed. With eight years of friendship under our belt, she knew me far too well.)

I felt dragged further into the mud every time Declan reached out to casually say hello, only to suddenly disappear again a day or two later. I wanted this back-and-forth nonsense to stop. And for it to stop now.

So I responded the only way I knew how, firm and direct:

"Hi Declan. Good to hear from you. Although in the past I've sugar-coated things, I think it's important that I be upfront with you this time. The first time you disappeared almost two years ago, I was devastated. The second time, a year ago, I simply tolerated it. This last time in December was a slap in my face. I'd love to be your friend but on one condition: You do not disappear whenever it's convenient. I will not put up with that anymore. I hope you understand."

"You're right. You're absolutely right." His texts were coming in faster than the breaking celebrity news I was waiting on.

"How can I make it up to you?"

"Well, for one thing, let's stop this messaging thing. It gets us nowhere. Call me whenever you want to talk."

Not a second sooner, my phone rang.

His voice, now my first time hearing it in two years, felt familiar and reassuring as that hot cup of latte I still had in my hand. Declan sounded confident and strong, but with an undeniable tinge of brokenness in his words.

"Heyyyy you. How have you been? It's definitely been a while since we spoke, and it's totally my fault. I'll be honest. I've thought about you and wanted to know how you're doing. But before we really get into things, there is something I need to tell you, Maíra" he began.

Although bothered by the fact that he hadn't even let me get a word in yet about how I was doing or what I was up to nowadays, I could sense something alarming in his voice, but I wasn't exactly sure what. I still resented him for disappearing two years ago out of the blue, and I still considered him a complete *idiot* for it.

"I don't know if you will want to be my friend after this," he cautioned. "But okay, I might as well tell you. So. Long story short. I met a girl online in December then married her in February – I know, call me crazy — and it has been the worst decision of my life. She was never right for me, and she turned out to be somebody completely different than what I thought, and I realized it a little too late. Everything recently came to a head and I'm at a loss on what to do."

Pause.

I was shocked. *What do you mean you got married?! To somebody after only two months of knowing them? Are you fucking kidding me?*

Marrying somebody on a whim was so unlike Declan. His first marriage with the mother of his daughter lasted ten years, so it wasn't something he ever took lightly. "Nobody will ever meet my daughter, not for at least a good year after I've been dating that person," he would say after his first divorce. Yet, that nobody turned out to be somebody he got hitched to two months after they first met.

I wanted to give Declan an earful and call him a fool, but I knew no good would come of it. For some odd reason or another, he was reaching out to me for support and I didn't want him to feel even worse than how he already did. *But how did he meet her? And why in the world did he think of taking on life with somebody only two months after knowing her?* Evidently, there was a lot more to the story, and it was an unraveling of stories within stories he would tell me when he was ready.

Later that day, once back in my apartment, I kicked off my *Havaianas* sandals into my cluttered bedroom closet then made myself a cup of tea and settled on my bed that still smelled of William before calling Declan back. We agreed we would talk more in the evening. This wasn't the type of conversation to have at a Starbucks anyway.

I looked around my bed and thought about all the junk I had left accumulate in my room recently. Magazines were hanging off my small trash can. Piles of work clothes sat on top of a wooden chair by the window. My dirty, stained socks from the gym had yet to be placed in the hamper. It was a good thing Declan was hundreds of miles away and couldn't see any of this.

"Hello?" Before I even had a chance to sit comfortably on my bed, Declan had already answered his phone.

"Hey, it's me," I said. "I'm home now. And all yours. Well, I'm here to listen, I mean." It was too soon for me to consider being even a bit flirtatious.

"So tell me," I continued. "How did all of this happen?"

I listened as Declan began telling me the story of how he and his second wife Ally met, and how it wasn't long before everything spiraled out of control. She was a school teacher in the suburbs of Roswell with two kids of her own, and only in her late twenties. Previously married like him, she and Declan met on the dating website Christian Singles. On the surface, she appeared to be your average woman looking for love, but Declan's description of her made me think of Cruella de Vil from *101 Dalmatians*. Manipulative at its finest and just all around crass.

"She's nice one minute, then completely verbally and emotionally abusive, Maíra. She's called me *faggot* and tried to hit me when mad more times than I can count, and she gets upset over the smallest things," he shared. "Her own sister warned me of her when we first met – said she was bad news

– but I didn't listen. I took the plunge and still decided to marry her only after two months. I know what you're thinking, *what in the world were you thinking?* And that's still something I'm trying to figure out myself."

I wasn't exactly surprised at his impulsive decision to marry this so-called Ally monster. I always kind of knew Declan to be a bit impulsive. I mean, for starters he hadn't disappeared out of my life because he gave it good thought. And though I knew his impromptu marriage was something even a five-year-old child would have attempted to talk him out of, this false perception of love had made him blinder than a bat.

"You are the only one who knows about how bad my marriage has really been," he noted. "I feel like my world is falling apart and I can't believe I was such an idiot, but I'm already in the process of getting a divorce. It should be finalized within the next couple of months."

The shock of it all had yet to settle in. I was flattered that he was opening up to me, to an old friend of sorts. But I also couldn't avoid the obvious question, so I buckled and asked.

"Why are you confiding in me all this?"

"Because… I'm not sure," he said. "I guess because you are the only one who has never judged me. Even if it means I married somebody only two months after meeting them."

3

The Months In Between

Hot summer nights where I previously hit up my favorite hole-in-the-wall bars with friends soon turned into long, late-night phone conversations with Declan, toasting to a familiarity I never thought I would have again while drinking away the personal troubles that pained him. It was now June, only a month after he re-appeared out of nowhere and we started reconnecting; yet the passing of time had not changed how easy it was for us to pick up right where we left off, either. Just as it was in the beginning.

I always felt like I could tell Declan anything and everything that crossed my mind. The months now since his return were no exception. Whether it was laughing with him about the rather interesting tale of a military guy I once dated who talked out loud to his GPS (*"Yes, Suri. Thank you. I'll make a left here"*) or bemoaning about the ongoing everyday frustrations of paying bills (*"Ugh. I have so much credit card debt this month"*).

Declan insisted I indulge him with the current happenings of my day-to-day life, no matter how mundane or outrageous. It would make him not think about his own life for a little bit, and anything could have been welcomed as a much-needed relief from his divorce drama at this point.

So I told him about how I was settling into my new home in Broward, my very first one-bedroom apartment off University Drive. I still lived in Miami the last time we saw each other, but during my delayed mid-quarter life crisis, a stark, positive change in my life was in immediate order. Broward became that place for me. Here I could find my independence every time I stepped outside and looked up at the tall palm trees, swaying in the breeze, on these paradise city streets that would put others to shame.

I was also closer to my dad, who now only lived ten minutes away, in the city of Sunrise, just north of Plantation. He was approaching his seventies yet you would never know it. Sharp as a whistle, dad could talk to you for hours on end about his latest book reads concerning Buddhism and Spirituality, or the best *cortadito* he found down the road at a Cuban gas station.

It had also been four years since my mother unexpectedly passed away due to several health ailments, and being there for my father, who was going through his own health ailments, became the number one priority for me. I could rest easy knowing I was nearby for his chemo sessions. Stage 4 had been a part of our lives for seven years now, and the fact that I could quickly scoop up my dad whenever he needed me and take him to doctor visits provided us both much-needed relief. There was no more driving for a good 45 minutes just to reach him. 45 minutes that, in a dire situation, could prove to be 45 minutes too late.

I was around Declan's daughter's age when my parents divorced, just a pre-teen myself. And when my mother passed in 2012, life as I knew it, forever changed. So it was just me and dad now. Like Bella, I, too, was an only child, and I understood the special bond and love we never cease to feel as daddy's little girl.

From the moment I could talk, my dad made sure to instill in me the value of growing up to be an independent woman. I was only two years old when he uprooted our small family from Brazil to the United States, in order to have a better life. Mom had been in and out of the hospital in São Paulo since I was born a premature baby at only seven months, so when dad received the opportunity to take his banking career overseas, he jumped on the chance. That's when we settled in Miami. With nothing to our names, just a dream and everybody's hopes for a better life combined into ours.

I spent most of my childhood in Miami, with stints of living in Grand Cayman and London here and there as well. Then, when I was 11, my parents divorced, and the mayhem of experiencing what I considered to be my first life-devastating event ultimately changed the child in me. But dad was determined to treat me no differently post-divorce, even if we no longer saw each other as often now due to my mom's jealousy and insistence on keeping me all to herself.

When dad and I did get together, however, I was home. I could talk to him about my first serious boyfriend in high school and how I lost my virginity at 16 without the fear of reprimand or judgment. I could cry in my dad's arms when my mother treated me badly and called me *worthless*. I knew I would be okay every time dad wiped the tears away from my then still pitch black hair to remind me I was everything but. "Maíra, you are not a reflection of your mother," he would say.

When I was around my father, I felt like I could get through anything. But if he was hurting, too, I would have never known. He was the first to put on a smile and tell me how much he loved me, just as Declan did with his own daughter.

Declan knew about my inner turmoil and teenage hardships and more. He, too, had dealt with his share of disappointments and bouts of conflict with his own mother. Back when we first met, we would spend hours confiding in each other like we were in search of a lifelong therapist to help us get through, so it was natural that we eventually grow to become the closest of friends for a period of time. But now, talking to him about the everyday occurrences of my life and most recent move to Broward felt silly. None of it could compare to the ever-growing stress Declan faced.

I could tell he just wanted this pending second divorce to be over and done with. In addition to the emotional abuse, his soon-to-be-ex wife *numero dos* had left him in a money pickle of a situation. The sky-rocket attorney bills, the court fees, the joint credit card drama and other discombobulated legal matters were clearly putting Declan between a rock and a tight spot. With his financial life in shambles, filing for bankruptcy seemed like the only logical solution to all these woes.

"Relationships are so complicated," I muttered while exhaling my grape-flavored e-cigarette during one of our now regular, day-to-day phone chats. Sitting barefoot on my bed with a fresh coat of polish on my toenails, the swirling smoke around me started to put me in a pensive frame of mind. Enough for me to start uttering my random thoughts out loud. I thought about what Declan was doing on the other side of the line, in Georgia. Maybe he was secretly smoking one of his favorite clove cigarettes as we spoke, or maybe he was fully tuned in to whatever ramblings were causing havoc inside my brain.

"I mean, dating alone is a rollercoaster ride, and God knows I've had my share of wild adventures," I said, while fascinated by the little zig-zag line of cigarette smoke that moved seamlessly in the air.

"Oh yeah? Hopefully you never felt like it was wild and crazy with me," said Declan. I could tell I had his full attention, just by the simple notion of anything being potentially *wild*.

"With you, it was only wild and crazy in a good way, silly. But you wanna hear a crazy-what-the-fuck dating experience I had a while back, though?"

"Give it to me."

"Well, okay. So one time I dated a guy – let's call him Eddy – who asked me once if I wanted a lick. You can imagine I had no idea what he was talking about – a lick of ice cream? A lick of a lollipop? What? Until a few seconds later it finally dawned on me that he wanted to know whether or not I wanted him to go down on me. You following me so far? But who the fuck says, 'do you want a lick?' And yes I swear to you those were his exact words."

"You've got to be kidding me. No fucking way!" Declan's roaring laughter could be heard so loudly over my phone, I almost had to pull my receiver away.

"I swear to you. That's what happened. Sex is fun and all – but talk about a total turn off when you put it like that. This guy needs a 101 on How Not To Kill The Mood."

"Aww. I feel bad for him. So does that mean I can't give you a lick?" teased Declan. His endearing voice was light and playful now.

"You – well, hmm. We'll have to see about that, mista."

"Ha! Oh really now? I see how it is. On a serious note, though – guess what – so I recently made a crazy decision. Well, it's not crazy for me but to others it might be."

"What's that?"

"Well, I've decided I'm gonna go a full year without sex. It's a promise I've made to myself. Just pure celibacy and I'm sticking to it. Ex *numero dos* just fucked with my emotions and now I feel like I have a hard time trusting women, period. I don't know if I'll ever allow myself to be vulnerable again. So no sex for me! Zip! Nada!"

"Wow. A full year? Are you sure that's what you want?" I asked, feeling confused by such a sudden and unexpected revelation.

"I'm more sure than I've ever been before," Declan responded confidently.

"Well then, props to you. I support your decision. Can't say I would do the same if I had a choice. But with everything you have going on, I completely understand your reasons for wanting to do this."

I wasn't sure if Declan had lost his mind or if he was making one of the smartest, most emotionally-sound decisions of his life. Even though I dare say I felt it was a bit on the impulsive side. I couldn't say I agreed with his decision, but who was I to judge. He was still struggling to come to terms with his divorce, and how "fake" his ex-wife was as he described her. If celibacy is what provided him relief, I wasn't going to get in his way.

While still on the topic of relationships, I thought I would take the opportunity to dig a little deeper. After all, who doesn't like some brain picking from time to time?

"Okay. I've got a semi-random question for ya. You ready? How do you know when you've found the right one?" I pondered out loud. By now I was up to the third coat of red polish on my nails – even though I knew it was a bit excessive – but with no more puffs left to exhale from my e-cigarette, I needed something else to keep my anxiety at bay.

"Ha! And you're asking me?" laughed Declan. "Hmm. You know what. In all honesty, I think a pastor once said it to me best. This is what he said. He said that you have to ask yourself, 'Am I the guy that the girl I am looking for is looking for?' Stop to think about that for a second. Are you the person the person you're looking for is looking for, too? I know, it's a bit of a tongue twister. Sometimes we just don't know right away. Chemistry, of course, also has a lot to do it with it."

"I believe that too," I said. "But you know, if one little thing doesn't align or it's not the right time or whatever, forget it. There's practically no chance."

He paused for a moment. "Yeah, guess you're right. Hey, I want you to know something while I have you on the phone. I enjoy our talks, you know that. I always have."

I wondered what prompted this random stream of consciousness. Had this conversation taken place in person, I imagine we would have been smiling at each other while he played with my often-tangled hair and I counted the precious wrinkly dots on his face.

"I enjoy our talks as well," I reassured him. "I know you're going through so much right now but you'll get through it. I'll do what I can to help you see the light of day again."

"Thank you. You have no idea how glad I am that we're talking again. And I'll be honest with you. Most people bore me," he continued. "But not you, Maíra. You are not – and never have been – *most people*."

"I love you."

Half-asleep, the alarm on my cell phone buzzed me out of sweet slumber with a text message notification, only mere hours after Declan and I wrapped up our philosophical conversation with tangents of unrequited love and everything in between. The quiet darkness of the night had me warm and snug under the covers, and I just wanted to stay in bed. But I groggily turned on my nightstand light to see a text message with those three words staring back at me.

I smiled. It was that type of smile you never want to get over, wishing you could make that feel-good sigh out of your chest last forever. It was the second time in the months since Declan returned that he said those words to me. But I knew better than to think anything of it. From one friend to another, he was merely being well... *a friend*.

"I love you more," I wrote back.

Several hours passed before either of us said anything to each other. It was as if we were just basking in those moments of uncertainty and sweet tenderness that often spoke to the both of us so well.

4

4th of July (II)

In those early summer months of May to June, Declan became a consistent denominator again in my life. Out was William, and in was the one I never thought I would hear from again.

Declan and I talked every day, and every day he updated me on how he was doing, as well as how the divorce proceedings and financial issues were playing out. Just like old friends, you would have never thought any time had passed between us all.

It was now the morning following that unexpected 4th of July Monday when I got out of bed, just as the Georgia sun began to rise and the clouds parted to reveal clear skies. There was something about this Peach State that spoke to me and always made me feel at home. I was embraced by a comforting silence I did not typically find in South Florida. Every person I met was less of a stranger and more of a friend, one you could have a natural yet enveloping conversation with, as you would with a close loved one you held near.

Daylight started to bounce off the walls in his daughter's bedroom, nudging me to get up and get a move on, as I reluctantly tried to wake up. I wondered what it looked like outside. Glancing through Bella's glitter-covered bedroom window, I could see her trampoline in the backyard. A cheerleader at her junior high school, the trampoline marked the epitome of fun and a carefree life for any young girl.

Nature here spoke to me, too. The bald cypress trees in Declan's backyard weren't like any we had in Florida. Big and bushy, several of them outlined the fence in his backyard where the grass was untamed and a lawnmower sat in the corner, collecting dust. I wanted to stare outside the window for hours on end, just imagining the grilled-charcoal smell of summer BBQs while envisioning the bursting fireworks display at night. But the reality of things was different. This trip was made on a much more somber and personal note.

I knew it would be a few hours before Declan awoke and poked his head in Bella's room to say *good morning,* or remembering how late he often slept, it could even be afternoon before then. "Do you recall that one time you woke up at one in the afternoon, and I was so nervous something was wrong, I even texted my friend, asking her what to do?" I later asked him. He couldn't remember the incident from two years ago. "You should have just woken me up," he joked.

"You? Wake you up? I have better luck waking up Godzilla than you, silly," I joked back.

24 hours. I only had 24 hours to talk to him and hope that he would see everything would be okay. He did not have to suffer like this. There was no reason for a man to feel trapped by his own thoughts.

I grabbed my warm, fuzzy jacket and made my way downstairs, tip-toeing on the edge of a long-winding staircase that led to the hallway right by Declan's office, next to an overflowing laundry room. The A/C inside the office room felt cool on my shoulders, even with the thermostat set on 75 degrees. I still couldn't get over how big the house was for just him and Bella, but the sheer size of this place I considered a mansion of sorts made you feel welcomed in its majesty.

After Declan's recent separation from ex wife *numero dos,* I hadn't even seen him walk into any of the four empty rooms, aside from his master bedroom and that of Bella's during my stay. There was no trace of his ex wife's presence here. The last remaining evidence of her – an Amazon box with some of her KitchenAid belongings to mail out – stood by his front doorstep. It was clear Declan wanted this woman's existence wiped from his memory.

Boxes full of printing paper, school yearbook pictures of Bella looking as happy as can be, and miscellaneous items I couldn't make out for the life of me took up most of the office space. I could tell this was yet another room Declan didn't really care to hang out in. It was just as out of balance and unclear as his unfocused mind.

Standing outside the office door, Declan's Australian Cattle dog jolted out of his peaceful sleep as soon as he saw me fumbling through a stack of white papers, anxiously wagging his tail and waiting to see if I'd fill up his food bowl that now sat empty from the night before. Declan's first wife, Bella's mom, had found Ozzy one evening roaming the streets of Marietta, looking somber and alone. He was little then, no bigger than a tote bag, and his searching eyes were enough for her to bring him home. Eight years later, after the settlement of the first divorce, Ozzy now turned to Declan to care for him as both his mom and dad.

I poured some chicken and brown rice nibblets into Ozzy's bowl from the six-pound dry food bag Declan kept stocked up in his pantry. Once Ozzy heard the rumbling of food, I was out of his radar and free to start my hunt for some more pen and paper. I had something up my sleeve. I wanted to write down any kind of uplifting thoughts that would perhaps make Declan feel okay but I wasn't sure what to write.

With so many office supplies around me, I didn't know where to look, but there by Declan's desk I found a pack of untouched printing paper and a couple of gel black pens. Since I was a child, for no reason I could explain, I often felt superstitious about writing in blue ink. So a black pen would do.

Ever so quietly, I then made my way back up to Bella's room, hoping Ozzy wouldn't create a scene and follow me. I found a comfortable spot by a couple of big-smiling stuffed animals, so I opened up the ruffled curtains and pulled up the browser for Google Chrome on my Android phone. I wondered what I could say to somebody who needed hope restored in his life.

Unable to draw any inspiration of my own, I searched for quotes and passages that may have resonated with Declan. *C'mon, Google. Help a girl out here.*

I also thought about how it would only be appropriate to draw inspiration from the most famous book of all: the Bible. Since I grew up turning to God during some of the most difficult times of my life, I hoped Declan would find comfort in doing the same.

Like many kids, I grew up in a Catholic environment, swaying to and fro between private religious schools, but if I were to be honest, I wasn't the type of girl who kneeled before the cross at mass service every Sunday. I didn't even go to mass on a regular basis, period. Some days God and I were close, while other days I wanted nothing to do with Him. Much like an ex you sometimes wish would just leave you alone. My faith only became stronger through several life-changing experiences I couldn't find any rhyme or reason for, including God's restoration of my relationship with my mother.

When my mother passed away, nobody saw it coming. It was a surprise to everyone who loved her. Yet, one of my biggest fears was that she would someday die without knowing how much she meant to me. The last time we ever saw each other, mom was in the hospital, just a couple of days into starting dialysis for kidney failure. Since the weather had surprisingly dropped down to a cool 60, I found myself waking up with a bit of a sore throat and a case of the sniffles the last day I went to see her at Mercy Hospital, one of the most well-known hospitals in all of Miami. Not wanting to get my mom sick, I stayed at the hospital only long enough to make sure she ate lunch and that the curtains were drawn for her afternoon nap, then I promised to return the next day.

"Mom, I'm getting sick. It's probably not a good idea for me to be around you like this. But I'll be back tomorrow so we can talk more then, okay? I love you," I said, before leaving the ICU room to then meet up with my best friend Oceana for our afternoon hangout in Broward.

That night, after enjoying an airbrush tanning session with Oceana, we were about to pull up to my dad's house in Sunrise. The clouds were closing in, and in just a few seconds it began to thunder outside. Not wanting to mess up our spray tan, Oceana and I decided to wait a few minutes in the driveway, inside her car, until the rain gave way. "Let's just give it a bit before we go inside," I said. I didn't even have to look at her to know she agreed.

Since the moment we met, Oceana was like the sister I always grew up wishing I had. Through a local Meetup event in Broward a few years back, we hit it off the second she gave me a ride to an icebreaker gathering for those looking to socialize and form lifelong friendships.

Originally from Peru, Oceana's flowy black hair and exotic figure was enough to make anybody feel captivated by her beauty. Like myself, she, too, was an only child. We were women in our twenties when we met, figuring out life and trying to find ourselves again after difficult breakups. Whenever I was feeling down, she became the first person I turned to, and without hesitation, she always had alcohol or ice cream ready to shoo my blues away. She was also the only friend I had who lost a parent. I couldn't have predicted God's perfectly orchestrated timing to make sure she was with me the moment the doctor called to give me the news.

The rain started to pour heavily now, and I wondered how much longer we would have to wait before we could make a run for it into my dad's dry and warm living room. Then, my phone rang.

"What the hell, my mom's hospital is calling me. Why in the world would they be calling me when I was just with my mom earlier today?"

"That's weird. There's no reason for them to call you. This can't be good…." Oceana could tell something was seriously wrong.

"Hello?" I answered.

"Maíra, I need you to come to the hospital right now," the doctor stammered. I didn't even know his name but I knew by the tone of his voice he wasn't playing around.

"Why?" I asked, wanting further details. "Doctor, I was just there with my mom. Did something happen? What is going on?" I could sense a deep sigh and trapped hesitation forming in his throat.

"Well, we don't typically share this over the phone, but your mother is dead. She just had a heart attack."

Just like that. There was no *"I'm sorry to inform you, but."* No *"I'm sorry to have to break this to you, but."* Cold and short and to the point is how I found out my mother had passed.

I was only 28.

But even with the passing of time, I needed my mother still and I needed God. And I knew, in the deepest corners of his heart, Declan needed Him too.

I took my spontaneous trip to Georgia as a sign that I needed to be here. Whether or not there was, in fact, a divine plan behind these sudden synchronicities and coincidences didn't matter. What mattered was that I was here with Declan. Even if it meant seeing him at his most vulnerable stage.

Okay, God, I'm listening.

With thirty scribbled notes of inspirational quotes down – and my right hand about to go numb – it was time to stop writing. 30 quotes for 30 days. Each sheet of paper contained a faith-filled or hope-based reminder of some sort, both from the Bible and my most trusted friend named Google. While many consisted of common sayings such as *This too shall pass* or *Faith can move mountains,* at this point I reckoned anything could have been regarded as a saving grace.

"Hey! How long have you been up?!"

I turned my head to find Declan peering into his daughter's sunshine-lit room as I glanced at him bright-eyed and pleasantly surprised that he was up early – it was still morning!

"Hey you! Oh, just a few hours," I said, trying to hide the notes behind me. I would give these to him later.

"Did you have any breakfast?" he asked, now inching closer to me with his sweet, bedroom stare. "I can cook you up something if you'd like – maybe some scrambled eggs and sausage – and then we can hang out and talk."

I didn't care much for breakfast, really. I just wanted to spend every moment with him.

I followed Declan downstairs (this house was a constant maze of up and down, up and down) as he treated himself to a protein shake in the kitchen and I grabbed a peanut-butter-and-jelly sandwich in the fridge. With our breakfast treats in hand, we then made our way to the adjacent living room where Ozzy's eyes suddenly perked up, just waiting to see what food of ours he could take a bite of.

A glass coffee table in front of us was covered with bills and unopened letters, along with a Bible in the center. Made of leather, the pages hinted trimmings of gold with a "WWJD" bookmark inside. "My friend gave that to me," said Declan, noticing my curiosity and firm gaze.

So much time had passed since Declan and I bonded over our faith the first time we met. Over the years, he, too, experienced his share of good days and bad days with God, but I wondered if the recent turn of events made Declan want to seek Him once more.

The shakeup of his short-lived marriage gone wrong was traumatic enough to make him question how and why he kept making poor decisions for himself, as well as question why he chose to be with someone who, in turn, also treated him badly. Like the time ex wife *numero dos* made him feel less of a man and compared his looks to others she deemed better looking. Or the time she called him names and the word *faggot* reverberated in his ears.

Now in hindsight, Declan theorized he married on a whim because he was simply trying to compete with his first wife who eventually remarried. But blinded by so-called love, jumping into a second marriage without giving it a second thought seemed like the sound thing to do. At least at the time.

Sunday morning. July 3rd. Declan arose with one objective in mind. The struggle was real, and the fight was no longer worth fighting for. How could he continue fighting when he was backed into a corner, time and time again. Every day, a new problem. Every day, a new issue to resolve. Every day he saw a pile of dominoes perfectly stacked against each other, just waiting for the right moment to topple over in a sudden, loud crash. His first and second marriages were both failures. He was helpless and alone.

But the car in his garage was running. He could climb inside, close the driver seat door and put his mind to rest. In an instant carbon monoxide would get the job done, he told himself. Here, Declan did not have to think or worry about anything or anyone anymore. Here, in this moment, he could set himself free. He did not want his daughter Bella to ever see that woman again. A woman who was the stuff evil stepmoms are made of. No! What if Bella had to see her again? No. No. That was one thing he could not let happen. His burden was his to bear, but it wasn't his daughter's. That was enough for him to get out of the car and surrender to the tiny hope that he still had a life worth living.

Ignition, off.

It was only a moment later that his name – and that disconcerting text – flashed on my cell phone. "Maíra, I appreciate all you have done for me during this whole mess, I really don't know how I would have made it this far. Just know that I love you."

And now I was here. Face to face with the man I deeply cared for.

Okay, God, once again, I'm listening.

"Have you been reading the Bible?" I asked, flipping through the pages of the Word of God and sitting comfortably with one of my hands on Declan's lap.

"I'm trying to again. I would like to read it with you sometime if that's okay."

"Of course. Whatever you'd like," I smiled. "I've actually been listening to several modern Christian songs lately that really speak to me. Do you

remember when we used to listen to them together? What was that song...
that one song by Building 425 that was your favorite?"

"Hmm. *We Won't Be Shaken?*"

"That's it! That's the one. You liked that song so much."

Searching through my Christian music Spotify playlist on my phone,
I looked for the song I remembered Declan once saying is what got him
through the hard times. We won't be shaken was a motto he lived by then.
Perhaps this time was no different.

*Whatever will come our way, through fire or pouring rain, we won't be
shaken. Whatever tomorrow brings, together we'll rise and sing. Because we will
trust in You and we will not be moved, and no, we won't be shaken.*

I could tell the melody of the song brought a sense of peace and comfort
neither of us had felt in a long time when his eyes suddenly began to well up
with tears. "I had not heard that song in so long. I almost forgot how much
I loved it," he said, setting his deep-set, dark eyes on mine. "Thank you for
reminding me of it."

"Of course, sweetie," I said, caressing his thigh. "Sometimes we all just
need a little something to make us feel less alone."

Time was quickly creeping up on us now and we hadn't even realized it.
With only five hours to ourselves before my required check-in at the airport,
I would soon have to leave and thus struggle to say goodbye once more.
So we did all we could do with the time left: We cried and we prayed and
we worshipped together, and we also spoke from the heart. Just as you do
when you've kept things trapped inside for so long, you don't even notice the
streams of words and sentences that come out of your mouth as you desperately hope anybody will hear you.

"I've just been feeling so lost, Maíra," he suddenly sighed. "I don't know
how to get myself out of this rut. I have no money and I married a woman
I should never have had anything to do with. I was so foolish. I feel like this
divorce can't come soon enough."

I ached to see my friend in such a state of despair. This was the first time I had ever seen Declan feeling so low with hints of paralyzing depression creeping through. And as I held him, I wondered whether the glimmer in his eyes was a reflection of the light from the awfully-bright kitchen lamp, or if they were tears he was earnestly trying to hold back.

I wanted to simply wrap my arms around Declan and hold him close. Like a mother would a child. Like his own estranged mother never did with him growing up. We both seemed to have lived parallel lives when it came to our experiences with our mothers. While I often had to deal with my mother making me feel less than, and stopping me from seeing my father as often as she could, Declan also had to deal with a mother who was manipulative and controlling.

On one particular occasion that stood out from his childhood, Declan's mother was forced into psychiatric care. He could still vividly remember the cops showing up at his door and taking his mother away. "My mother was always crazy," he would say. "I don't think I ever saw her normal. Even my first ex hated her. She was as fake as they come, and she made both my brother and I suffer in her bitter, angry world. Even from an early age, I always felt like she was bipolar and I could never understand why my father stuck around. I think that's when I started losing my innocence too and kind of started to hate life."

Although there was nothing I could do for Declan in those last few moments before driving to the airport, except simply be present, I needed him to make me a promise. One he could not go back on, and one he would pinky swear to if he had to. While I had him face me on the couch, I looked up into his eyes, now red from such emotional distress.

"Sweetie, I understand that you're in pain. I understand that sometimes you feel so overwhelmed that it is only natural for darkness to set in and make itself known. But you cannot let it stay there. Please remember that you are stronger and better than any obstacle you face. Don't give your power away. Promise me you won't forget these things."

"I promise," he managed to whisper.

I still wasn't ready to get on my flight. I wasn't ready to return to the so-called normalcy of life that was anything but normal. Every time Declan shed a tear, I cried right along with him. And every time he shook his head in shame, I wanted to press my hand inside his chest and remove those feelings of guilt that made it hard for him to breathe. We had entrusted the past 24 hours onto each other, hoping for anything that gave us one more day to make it through, and I hoped more than anything that somehow we could.

The Hartsfield-Jackson Atlanta International Airport is considered the busiest airport in the United States, accommodating more than 100 million passengers every year. Finding your gate the first or second time is much like trying to find an exit doorway to a maze that has too many baggage cart obstacles and crowds of people who just seem intent on getting in your way. Although the line at the security checkpoint wasn't long when Declan and I arrived, I knew I had to calculate a good twenty to thirty minutes to get to my gate. Thankfully, we made it just in time for me to do one final check of my belongings. *Wallet, check. Driver's license, check. House keys, check. Car keys, check. Flight ticket, check.* Hovering over me, Declan stood patiently as he watched me go through my imprinted tote bag, throwing out old receipts and sorting through the essential items I needed on hand. Lip balm included. He was wearing one of his favorite Minions shirt with a grey cap on and a pair of faded blue jeans that had me wishing I could stay for just an extra day.

"You got everything?"

"Yes, I think so. You gonna be okay, hun?" I asked.

"I'm gonna be okay. Just you taking the time to fly out here last minute meant everything to me. All I can say is thank you."

Declan's grey cap was now turned backwards, and I kept trying to smooth out the crinkles of my floral blouse that accentuated my curves. For a moment, Declan stood before me, leaning his almost six-foot-tall frame to be at eye level with me. Like a little boy, he looked at me lovingly, and like a little girl, I stood before him on my tippy-toes. Not quite ready to leave. Never thinking, never believing, that two years later I'd be here again.

"I'm so glad you came, Maíra. I mean that. Even if just for 24 hours. You're the best for doing this for me."

He didn't need to say anything more. His dreamy dark eyes were enough to grab me and pull me in for that long-awaited kiss I had been thinking about since the night before. And this time, I wasn't about to turn away.

PART II –

Falling
In Deep

"What if I fall? Oh, but my darling, what if you fly?"

— Erin Hanson

5

Fireproof

"There is a movie I recently saw that I just know you're going to love," insisted my co-worker, Greg, during one of our lunch-break walks around the block from our Wynwood office. I had been back in South Florida for a week now, getting back to my regular everyday routine, while Declan and I toyed with the idea of me visiting again during an upcoming weekend we both had free.

"Oh yeah? I asked intrigued. "What's it called? What's it about?"

"Well, it's a Christian movie from the same creators of *War Room* that you've seen and liked. It's called *Fireproof*, with Kirk Cameron. It's a love story, really. About a firefighter who wants to save his relationship so he learns about this thing called a Love-Dare challenge. For 40 days he has to demonstrate 40 different acts and gestures of love. It's a pretty neat concept. Especially since we often don't take the time to put in the effort to show the ones we love how much we love them."

"Wow. That sure does sound interesting. And yup, I definitely agree with you. We hardly ever take the time at all to show how much we care. "

"They even have a book about the Love-Dare challenge for those who want to do it for their girlfriend or boyfriend, or husband or wife. But there is one catch."

"What's that?"

"You can't tell them you're doing it while you're doing it."

"Ooh, and the plot thickens! I'll have to watch the movie and check out the book, too."

"I know they have a free PDF online with the basic day-by-day instructions of how to follow the challenge. I can send you the link if you want. I also have a copy of the movie. I can bring it in tomorrow, so you can watch it over the weekend."

"Sounds like a plan!"

Greg, who grew up in Haiti and often drove a motorcycle to work, was only one of two friends who shared the same Christian faith I did. Oftentimes he would send me a YouTube video of a worship song that recently spoke to him. Other times he'd get excited telling me stories about the young kids at his church camp, who were learning to trust the Word of God. In many ways, we shared the same views, and we also loved the same movies. *War Room* being one of them. So when he recommended I check out *Fireproof* too, I knew his positive reviews of it would deliver.

With the borrowed copy of Greg's DVD in hand, I invited my father over on a Friday for a popcorn-and-movie-night in. He would provide the wine and I'd provide some fun, bonding time with his daughter, as well as some slobbery kisses from his grandson – my six-year-old Toy Shih Tzu.

As a spiritual man himself who meditated in his room every night before bed, dad appreciated movies that made us think outside the box. There is always something we can learn and gather wisdom from that is greater than us he would say.

Dad arrived at my place early in the evening, ready to say hello to his cute four-legged grandson, while I got a couple of buttery kettle popcorn bags underway in the microwave. He looked so cute with his sombrero hat on and a pair of shorts that showed off his shapely, fit legs.

Every day before sunrise, dad was the first to get up to venture on a brisk, morning walk in his neighborhood and take in the sights and sounds of a new day. Approaching his seventies, his white hair was thinning now as a result of his weekly chemo, but nothing could stop dad from taking care of his health and marching ahead. Even when his glasses would fog up due to the heavy humidity outside, his life motto remained: One foot in front of the other, one day at a time.

"Hey dad! So glad you came. How was your day? Ready to watch this movie?"

"Hey, my Iazinha!" exclaimed dad, as he made himself at home with Lumee jumping up and down for grandpa to hold him.

"Sure am. You know I like watching faith-based movies. Oh! And I brought us some *pastelitos* and cookies, and I know you like wine, so here you go. Only $2.99 at Walmart. Can you believe that?!" Just like his daughter, dad was all about the bargain deals at the grocery store.

Once I could no longer hear a millisecond of a popping sound in the microwave, I poured our hot, buttery popcorn into a couple of small bowls and joined dad on the couch.

"Here, dad. Rest your feet up on this extended leg rest," I said, pulling out a leg rest contraption that was knee high. "You'll feel more comfortable watching the movie this way. Shall we begin?"

"Mmmm. This popcorn is good! I may get some more in a little bit... Oh, the movie – right. Yes, go ahead and hit play! Let's hope it's just as good as this popcorn."

Just a little over two hours, *Fireproof* was not too long and not too short. The characters felt like real people you could connect with, and the further the storyline progressed, the more I found myself engrossed by the beautiful layers of the movie. Kirk Cameron's performance was enough to put me on the edge of my seat with his true-to-life portrayal of a man at a crossroads in his life, as he is trying to keep his marriage together even in the midst of everyday life challenges. Until one day he learns about something called the Love-Dare challenge that changed his father's life – a challenge that requires you to show your love and devotion for your spouse for 40 days – and he decides to follow suit.

Interwoven with tales of both love and heartache, the movie explores themes of martial frustrations and sacrifices that we make in the name of love. And with a resounding emotional soundtrack to tie it all together, I was in a heap of tears by the time the end credits started to roll and I had used up all the toilet paper in my bathroom.

Equally as moved (though not to the point of crying a river like me) was my dad. All because *Fireproof* was simply put, exceptionally life-affirming and inspiring, and unlike any other movie we had ever seen before.

"Gosh. That was beautiful. I certainly wasn't expecting that," sighed dad, offering his handkerchief for me to dry my eyes once the movie finished playing, and the moonlit sky lit up in the distance.

"You're not kidding. What a movie. My god. It takes the meaning of unconditional love to a completely different level, huh."

I got up and poured dad another bowl of popcorn, as I treated myself to some more wine.

"Yes, *filha*. In life we eventually learn that real love is about sacrifices."

After overcoming so many challenges, my father still always knew best.

I knew in that moment that I wanted to take on the Love-Dare challenge, just as it was portrayed and described in the movie. But not for any no-good reason or just because. I felt something growing inside of me that I could no longer fight or deny. There was no escaping this love that began to overtake me in the most humbling yet beautiful of ways – and I wanted to show Declan that my love for him was a choice. Just as it had been two years ago, and as it still permeated and lived inside of me still. I wasn't going to give up the man I loved.

After my recent trip to Georgia, my friendship with Declan turned sacred. Sacred enough that his well-being became one of my top priorities, and our close bond fostered new hope. But there were also days when I could tell he continued to feel tormented by negative self-doubt, and his self-confidence slowly began to shatter in front of him.

Once considered the popular jock at his high school in Melbourne, Florida, Declan hardly had any real friends to call his own as an adult, even after living in Georgia for almost twenty years. Life kept getting the best of him, and I couldn't shake off the thought that I had also seen Declan hanging by a thread – and *it killed me.*

I wanted to walk through the fire and show him that he didn't have to go through it alone. Just like in *Fireproof.* Was I about to proclaim the ultimate declaration of love? Absolutely. Was it a really dumbass and naïve move on my part? Yup. Quite possibly so it was probably that, too.

It was rounding off midnight when dad decided to kiss me goodnight and bid me adieu after our marathon movie night. Sitting down for a straight two hours to watch a movie was not something dad was accustomed to any-more, especially with his draining and exhausting chemo sessions. Before he left, I offered to give him some leftover food that sat in my kitchen, so he didn't have to worry about cooking for himself or ordering takeout the next day. I felt thankful that dad had taken some time to spend the night with me and drive a good 20 minutes to my place – the last thing I wanted to do was make him stay longer. He looked tired and mentioned that he wanted to be in bed soon for another one of his early morning walks. I understood, and walked him to the door.

"Thanks for coming, dad. I always love watching these kind of movies with you. I feel like there's so much I can always learn, not just from the movie itself but from your own personal insights as well. You think you'll be good driving home?"

"I'll be fine. Don't stay up too late, *filha.* And give my grandson a kiss for me."

Lumee was already dozing off on my bed, curled up in his usual sleeping position and perhaps dreaming of new treats I would get him the next day.

"Thanks, dad. I'll check up on you tomorrow, okay? I love you."

"I love you too, Iazinha," he said kissing me goodnight. Closing the door behind him, I was then left to unravel the mystery and steps of the Love-Dare challenge. It was time to get started.

I pulled out my laptop, opened up my dusty screen and got online to begin my research. With a quick search of "Love-Dare Challenge," it seemed like a million different websites popped up – all with different explanations for how to complete this month-long dare. But although the instructions differed slightly from one website to the next, the concept remained pretty much the same for all: Complete 30 demonstrations of love for 30 days.

- *Day 1 – Give a compliment or say an encouraging word in the beginning of the day.*

- *Day 2 – Demonstrate patience by not saying anything negative. Patience allows the person you care for to be human. Patience gives you the ability to hold on.*

- *Day 3 – Show kindness in unexpected ways. Think of a loving gesture or act you can do for the person you love.*

- *Day 4 – Send something, such as a small gift, to show you were thinking of them.*

- *Day 5 – Ask how they are doing today. Genuinely show interest.*

Declan's birthday in August was just a little over a month away. I decided I would do the challenge to coincide and end right before his big day. Since he was also not my spouse, in some areas I would change certain dares and challenges as I saw fit. I would also use a scrapbook to chronicle the day-to-day events and undertakings of this unique yet heart-driven journey. Every day for 30 days. No matter what, I couldn't break. I had to be in. *All in.*

And there was one more thing: I couldn't tell Declan.

6

An Unexpected Passing

Towards the end of July, I booked a flight to visit Declan again in Georgia. Just as before, he would pick me up at the airport and then drive us to his home in Kennesaw. Although it hadn't been that long since I saw him last, it was enough for me to feel both physical and emotional pain at the thought of being hundreds of miles away from him.

Still tightly wrapped up in the legal matters of his pending divorce, Declan came up with a game plan to tackle any financial issues involving his ex. There were many lingering things to take care of, but with the attorneys of both parties handling most of it, that provided him some relief to try and resume his normal life. Everything seemed to be moving along, steadily under control.

And so I took the time to fully work on the Love-Dare challenge, spending my days catching up with Declan, while completing the challenge of the day behind the scenes. Like an obedient student, I was soon completely engrossed by all the love dares, making sure to write down the highs and lows of every experience in my scrapbook.

Day 10: Love is unconditional. Do something today or give a present that proves your love is based on your choice.

The day before my return flight to Atlanta I clocked out of work early to stop by Broward Mall and pick out my Love-Dare present for Declan. I wanted to give him something that held special meaning, and not just a random gift he could forget about and dump to the side in a week or two. I had heard that a store called *Things Remembered* was known for customizing gifts and adding a personal touch. I just needed to find that perfect present.

Traffic was not on my side as I made my way to Broward Mall and managed to get to the store only a little more than an hour before closing. I felt bad that Lumee had to wait longer than usual for his evening walk, but I only had 24 hours to find whatever I needed to for Day 10 of the Love-Dare and then head back to the airport once more.

Jessica, a sweet African-American lady who looked to be no older than her mid-thirties, met me as soon as I entered the store. Since it was nearing closing time, I was the only one there and thus was provided her full attention. With so many beautiful ornaments and mementos on display, I didn't know where to begin my search for the perfect gift.

"Good evening. May I help you?" asked Jessica.

"Hi – umm, yes, please. I'm looking for some kind of faith-based jewelry pendant that is designed for men. One with preferably a cross on it. In silver, too. If you have any."

"Of course, right this way, please," she said, taking me to the back end of the store. "We have several cross necklaces and chains here in this glass compartment. Gold, silver – do any of them interest you?"

I glanced my eyes over a large selection of shiny chains until one on the far right corner caught my eye. There, inside a small silver box with the name *Declan* engraved on it, was a silver cross pendant. *You've got to be kidding me.*

"What's this?" I asked, tapping my finger on the glass.

"Oh, that's a free jewelry box we give away with your purchase of $60 or more. We will also engrave it for you with any single word you'd like. As long as it's no more than six letters."

I didn't have to look any further. I was at the right place. After showing Jessica which silver cross chain I wanted, I requested that the name *Declan* be engraved on one side and *Psalm 117* on the other.

"Is this for a boyfriend?"

"It's for someone who means a lot to me."

"Of course. I just need you to now select the type of handwriting you would like us to use for the engraving."

Jessica then proceeded to pull out a printed sheet of paper with unique letterings and sample names from a hidden drawer tucked below the glass compartment. In calligraphy handwriting was the word *Bella*, the first name on the list. *Again, you've got to be kidding me.*

I was told the engraved etching would be done in half an hour, so I thought I could kill some time by calling Oceana and telling her about my little surprise gift. By now, Oceana had already had a change of heart about Declan, and seeing how happy I felt being reconnected with him was enough for her to be happy for me, too. Besides, I just had to share these one-too-many coincidences of the evening with someone who would understand.

"Oceana!" I exclaimed, stepping outside the store. "You're never going to believe this. I found Declan the most perfect present! And it was pretty eerie how I came across it, too. Almost like a sign!"

"Really? What happened? What did you get him?" she asked.

I told her about the chain, and the names, and how weird it was that I came across all of these things, in the same single store, at the same time.

"It sounds like somebody up there is looking out for you," she thought out loud.

I hoped she was right.

After Oceana and I hung up, I thought I would give Declan a quick call next and just keep the story about the gift to myself. It became common standard by now for one of us to either call or text the other at some point during the day and check in. But when his phone rang five times without an answer, I wasn't sure what to think. *That's odd. He usually answers right away. Maybe he's at the gym.*

"Miss Maíra, it's all ready for you." Jessica had found me standing on the corner of the store right as I was putting my phone away.

"Oh, great! Thank you," I said, placing the pendant in my hand and giving the smooth finish a thorough look. "It's really beautiful. You did an excellent job. I have to get going but I promise to be back sometime in the near future should I need something else."

"I'm glad you liked it and yes, please do," she said, smiling. "Make sure to come visit us again."

I could sense a headache coming on and felt pretty tired by the time I pulled up to my parking lot several minutes later and walked up to my doorstep. *Poor Lumee, I need to put on his leash and walk him right away before he pees inside the house.*

Clutching Declan's gift in one hand, I fumbled through my Coach purse with the other, trying to find my house keys in between lip balms and chewing gum that lay at the bottom. *Ah, here it is!* Just as I was about to turn the doorknob and run inside to take Lumee out for his walk, my phone rang. It was Declan finally returning my call.

"Hey! Talk about perfect timing! You always call me at the right time. I just got home. Wait until I tell you about my shopping adventure —" I said, rambling enthusiastically.

"No, Maíra. Not right now. You need to cancel your flight. You can't come up here anymore. I – I – My brother... *Oh my god. My brother!*"

I could hear the exasperation in Declan's voice, the trembling stutter in his attempt to string any two-or-three syllable words together. *Something was very, very wrong.*

"Declan, honey. What?! What about your brother? Did something happen? What's going on?!"

"My brother is dead," he cried. "My brother is deaaddd!"

I immediately dropped my purse, leaving Lumee unable to control his bladder any longer and wet the welcome mat on my doorstep.

In a matter of 24 hours, Lumee and his toys were dropped off at my dad's house, and I was at the airport boarding a flight back to Georgia. There was no way I was canceling my flight – not at a time like this. Declan's brother, along with his parents, lived in Melbourne. Since it was too last-minute for Declan to schedule a flight, I offered to drive down with him the second I arrived. I wasn't about to let him make the overnight drive to Florida on his own.

Losing my mother, I knew that grief had the capacity to strip away even our basic ability to function. If I could hear how distraught Declan sounded over the phone, I could only imagine how he was acting in person. At the very least he was not certainly not acting like himself, and understandably so. This was not a time for Declan to be – or do – anything alone. So we agreed on one thing: I would fly up to Atlanta as originally planned, pick him up, and together we would make the long drive to his parent's house in Melbourne. Just eight hours south.

8:30 p.m. Journal Entry –

I'm on a plane to Georgia writing this journal entry. And instead of excited, I am just heartbroken. Last night, I found out Declan's brother suddenly passed away. I cannot even believe I am writing those words. Stunned and shocked. The past 24 hours have eaten me away. Today was Day 11 of the Love-Dare challenge. Requiring me to "do something today that meets a need of his." So I'm picking him

up to drive back down to Melbourne, Florida. This morning, Declan was doing
fine, just fine. All before we found out about this awful bit of news. It's crazy how a
day can start off with you feeling wonderful and then it can end with you thinking
you're in the middle of a nightmare. I never thought I would have to prove my love
for him at a time like this. Grief is a fucking bitch.

I hurried to meet Declan outside the Atlanta airport as soon as I landed right around 10 p.m. With a tank full of gas and Ozzy loaded up in the backseat of the car, we were ready to begin our long drive to Florida just a few minutes after I arrived. There was no visiting Kennesaw this time. I wanted to hug Declan tight and tell him how sorry I was that he was facing yet another devastating tragedy, but I knew no words could do him any good right now. Without a moment to fix my hair, or take out some cash from the ATM in case he needed it, we were both simply running against time. I hopped in the passenger seat of his BMW I knew all too well and offered a simple gesture of affection by slightly brushing my lips across his shoulder. He looked pale white and I wondered if he could manage the long drive ahead.

"Thank you for coming. You didn't have to do this. I'm sorry that I can't even think straight right now, but I appreciate you being here, Maíra," he said. "And you're right – I don't think I could have done this drive on my own. I just can't believe all of this…. First, this pending divorce from my crazy soon-to-be ex-wife, then bankruptcy I have to file for, plus the fear of losing my job, and now my brother is dead…. and I have to see my parents whom I haven't seen in two years. I feel like I'm going insane!"

The late July night sky was fully visible with a shower of stars, except for the light poles on the highway that sometimes hindered our view. I watched Declan as he cruised down State Route 300 and the airport terminal faded in the distance. I was facing him now, hearing the growing grief-stricken vibrations in his voice every time he spoke, and careful not to interrupt.

"I'm so sorry, honey. I'm so sorry," is all I knew what to say.

I did not know much about his brother, John, except that he was eighteen months younger than Declan and the envy of so many with his ocean blue eyes. John was also known to be so insanely smart he once created several parts of a maneuvering-type software for a military plane. As kids, the two boys grew up to be close but once in college, stints here and there with drugs started to get in the way. And by the time the two became adults, John and Declan were more distant than twins separated at birth. Or in other words, they were estranged. And though Declan hadn't been given much information about his brother's passing, by all accounts, it was unexpected. Just like my mother's.

Declan maintained a stoic look as we continued the drive down to Florida. He wasn't any bit himself, and I couldn't blame him. But I wanted to capture every look and emotion in his eyes. I wanted to better understand his tumultuous upbringing, and the difficulties both he and his brother faced as adults. There was so much I didn't know, but I knew this much: Their story wasn't made up of a picket-white fence and daisy flowers surrounding their front yard. Instead it was one marred by mental illness, drugs and a dysfunctional kind of love. Like in any other family, pain and resentment found its way here, and it was something Declan very much still held onto.

And then there was the fact that less than 10 hours from now, Declan would see his parents for the first time in years. Just like his relationship with his brother, they too, for the most part, were estranged.

"How do you feel about seeing your parents again after so long? Is there anything I can do to make you more comfortable upon seeing them?" I asked. His eyes were focused on the road ahead but his emotions were just brewing below the surface.

"It is what it is. I'm just going down there to do what I have to do for my brother – to do my part – and that's it," he responded in a matter-of-fact tone. "I know my niece and nephews will be excited to see me, and I just have to be the meditator between my mother and my sister-in-law Anne in order to get things done."

John and Anne had three young kids and were in the process of separation when Declan's brother passed away. Although there was an element of concern that Declan's mom and Anne would butt heads and simply lose it with each other, this was the time to put ego aside and come together. Even as separated as everybody was. Even if it was just for this one time. Because, as my father would say, sometimes it is better to be at peace than to be right.

7

Melbourne

I could barely keep my eyes open. Somehow the long night had remained steady through countless hours of deep conversations and the occasional hand holding. But now, only a couple of hundred miles away from his parents' house, I could tell Declan needed a break from all the driving, especially when I noticed he had suddenly become unusually quiet. So I offered to switch seats and get behind the wheel so he could rest.

Since it was the beginning of a presidential election season, I kept myself entertained by listening to radio jockeys debate back and forth about Donald Trump's and Hillary Clinton's campaign trails. And every time I switched radio stations, it seemed like another DJ continued to have a field day mocking one or both of the candidates.

Ozzy still slept quietly in the backseat, and Declan had by now reclined his car seat to go to bed himself. I focused on the road in front of me. The exit signs to the city of Melbourne weren't too far away now, with only an hour left to go. We were getting close when I started to notice my head slowly bobble to the side, and the radio chatter of who was going to become the next president fade away. Scared to completely doze off, I knew we had to switch seats again.

"Don't hate me, but I don't think I can keep driving. I'm so tired...." I moaned, waking up Declan just as he was about to fall asleep.

While Declan managed to drive for six hours straight, I felt terrible that I couldn't even get more than an hour under my belt without straining my eyes to stay awake. "It's okay," he chuckled, rubbing his eyes. "You've already done more than enough for me. I'll drive. We're almost there anyway."

It was 6 a.m. by the time we pulled up to his parents' driveway, off the side of an almost barren road with a number of luxurious mansions under construction. This was a new residential area from what Declan explained, and thus the hot commodity of the town. In fact, it was so new, not many people outside of Melbourne even knew about this neighborhood yet. There were also no private gates yet surrounding the homes, but each house came equipped with its own fenced-in swimming pool and high-tech alarm systems that were sure to keep any intruder away.

Hearing the key finally out of the ignition, Ozzy hopped onto the front seat, eager to get out and give his bladder a much-needed release. Once on the ground, he found a patch of bushes nearby, and lifted his left rear leg before going about his business. We had officially arrived.

I felt myself increasingly nervous about meeting Declan's parents. Not only was it my first time coming face-to-face with the parents I heard so much about, but it was also under less than ideal circumstances. *How should I approach them? What should I say?* I was all too familiar with the waves of grief after losing my own mother, but this was different. They had just lost their youngest son, John – and nothing could compare to a parent's grief.

Plus they didn't know their other son was suffering too. Declan kept his second marriage secret from a good number of people, including his parents. But now that the divorce was underway, he thought it would be okay to tell them at the right time. Whenever that was.

"Declan! My love!"

I patted my frizzy hair off my face as I got out of the car and made my way to his parents' front door. A large welcome sign in cursive handwriting hung overhead, and the glass double-door entrance looked so spotless and clean, you could see right through it and to a Sony HDTV that appeared turned on to early morning news in the living room.

His mother, Daisy, was the first to approach us, and the second her eyes met Declan's, she pulled him into a deep embrace, careful not to sob all over one of his other laundry-fresh Minions shirt. His father was equally as emotional to see his now only son. But Declan remained stiff as a brick and determined not to cry. While I had to be strong for him, he had to be strong for his parents.

In between pauses of tears, I extended my arms toward Declan's mom.

"I'm so sorry for your loss, m'am."

"Mom, this is Maíra. She's been with me since last night after she flew in to Atlanta to drive down with me here." Even in the heavy grief that surrounded us, Declan made it a point to introduce me with a brief description attached.

I was instantly surprised by how his parents took to me with such kindness, despite the fact that I was a stranger entering their home. They showed concern inquiring about our long drive, and empathized when we mentioned, though slightly awkwardly, that we were rather tired.

His mother, Daisy, originally from Spain – where Declan was "conceived" as she later made it a note to point out – was of short stature, like myself. She had perfect light brown curls that were still holding up rather well, even after an excruciatingly difficult day. And although she was of European descent, any hint of a Spanish-English accent had been lost long ago.

His father, Jeremy, on the other hand, came from a long line of American military veterans. He struck me as humble and meek, yet strong in his own right. A wispy moustache highlighted his face, and it gave definition to a man who likely lived a lifetime of unspoken events that no one would ever know about.

The two met during Declan's father's deployment in Spain. Not long thereafter the happy couple settled their lives in the States, where Declan – and later John – was born.

After proper introductions were made, I hugged his parents and took their hands in mine as a manner of once again offering my condolences. "I am so very sorry…" I whispered. Although I could not possibly fathom the profound depths of their grief, I needed to extend my small token of love and support, for whatever consolation it was worth.

"Thank you for everything you have done for our son," said Declan's mom, wiping away a tear on her long nightgown sleeve. Here she was, extending gratitude to somebody she didn't even know, even as she looked at me with deep sorrow in her eyes. I couldn't even – I was in awe.

"It's the least I could do," I solemnly replied.

The sunrise was beginning to make way for a new day, so the four of us agreed to sit down and chat in the afternoon once everybody had enough sleep. After all, there was no way providing solace to distressed, heartbroken parents could do good of any kind when we were walking zombies ourselves. Not wanting to inconvenience me, Declan was to stay in one guest room that had so much stuff you could barely walk in, while I was to stay in another room, more adequate for a female visitor, down the hallway. As for Ozzy, he wanted to sleep with his father, of course.

"Text me later in the morning when you're awake," I reminded Declan. He nodded, gave me a kiss on the forehead goodnight then closed the guestroom door behind him. His parents, too, had already made their way to their master bedroom after offering a glass of water for us to keep on our nightstands.

I couldn't wait to get to bed myself. A larger-than-life stuffed teddy bear, sitting on top of an intricately designed bed quilt, greeted me as I walked into my guest room. *Why, hello there, Mr. Teddy Bear.* I had never seen anything so big. So big, in fact, that there was only room for one of us on the bed. *Sorry, Mr. Teddy Bear, but tonight you're gonna have to sleep on the floor.*

I dropped my carry-on bag by a rusty armchair next to my queen-sized bed, removed my contact lenses, checked to see if my window binders were fully closed then slipped into some comfy pajamas. After driving for almost nine hours, Declan was safe and sound with his family, and presumably already sleeping away to the murmurs of his brown noise app. In less than a minute, I, too, was fast asleep, feeling some sense of momentary relief.

The delicate matters that needed to be tended to after John's death required an enormous amount of patience and care. As I knew well in the sudden passing of my mother, the burden of taking care of these matters would also be left to the next of kin.

On the drive down to Melbourne, I opened up to Declan about the responsibilities entrusted in me in the aftermath of my mother's death. Though every case is different, I knew that being mindful of settling basic matters would ease some of the overwhelming tensions his family felt.

Did John have any credit cards? Has anybody requested a death certificate? Has the Social Security Administration been notified? Did he have car insurance? Are all his bills paid off? Did he have any month-to-month payments? Are there any doctors that need to be contacted? Did he have a life insurance plan? Does Anne have paid Bereavement Leave at her job?

Granted, these questions did not fall into a pile of typical conversations anybody wants to discuss, but they were still important things to consider. Because just like it requires a village to take care of a child, the same can be said about grief. Nobody can do it alone.

Late in the morning, I slowly began to wake up from a deep slumber when I heard the rumblings of people clattering their way around the kitchen that was right next to my guest room. I could hear Declan speaking, and his mother's voice also seemed to echo in the distance. I decided I would stay in my guest room for an hour or so to offer some privacy and space to the family. But soon, the delicious aroma of a home-cooked breakfast of scrambled eggs and hot brewing coffee lingered into my room, and I could hear Declan and his parents talking about his brother. No, correction, all I could hear were the agonizing painful sounds of utter devastation and unfathomable tragedy.

"I can't believe he's no longer here! Why, God! Why did you take my son!"

My heart broke every time I heard Daisy wailing over the incomprehensible realization that she had lost her youngest son.

Only in his early forties, John's three kids would now grow up learning about their father who was taken from them way too soon.

"I know, mom. I know. I'm in shock myself."

There wasn't much Declan could do except try to console his mother with his presence. Then, as a way to calm her down from this all-consuming grief, Declan changed the subject matter to recent events in his own life, hoping it would temporarily relieve her from some of the heart-wrenching pain. But just when he thought diffusing the situation by changing the subject would help, it suddenly seemed to only make it worse.

"She did what?!! And you married this woman???" yelled his mother. "Oh, if I ever meet her, Declan…. You better pray I never meet her! Do you understand me!" Yup, it seemed like Declan had finally told his mom about his recent second marriage.

Daisy's voice loudly reverberated through the walls in the living room and up to the dangling crystal towel hooks in the bathroom next door to me. This was one moment I was not looking forward to. Not only was Daisy completely distraught by her youngest son's death, but now she was finding out that her oldest son married somebody who was, to put it in layman's terms… *well, psycho.*

"Yes, mom, I know. I don't know what I was thinking. But it's okay. It's fine. It's all over now," Declan reassured her. "I already filed for a divorce. I made a stupid mistake marrying her. But we need to talk about John and Anne, and the kids…. We need to talk about the memorial service… *Please, mom, listen to me."*

I took that as cue to try and provide some comfort to Declan and let him know I was awake.

"Morning. I hear your mom yelling. I know it's hard but be there for her as best you can. Just try to stay calm and patient. You can do this," I texted Declan from my room.

"Hey, I see you're up. You can come out if you want. I'm in the living room," he wrote back. *Yes, I know you're in the living room. I knew since I first heard the unavoidable exchange of shouting words, silly.*

With the green light from Declan to show my face, I took a light jacket from my carry-on and said a little prayer as I slowly began to emerge in the exquisitely sophisticated living room, optimally suited for parents about to retire.

On one end, Declan's mother was sitting with him at the fine dining room table, while his father, Jeremy, flipped through the pages of that morning's newspaper in his recliner. Who knew there was ever any kind of noteworthy news in a town as sleepy and quiet as Melbourne. Several hot cups of *café con leche* and freshly-sliced mangoes were spread out on the breakfast table.

"Mom set these aside just for you, for when you woke up," mentioned Declan.

"Thank you, Daisy. I appreciate you thinking of me." I still couldn't get over at how gracious and kind his parents were treating me, an unknown guest.

"You're very welcome. Have I told you how *que bella tu eres,*" remarked his mother, as I noticed her affectionately smiling at me. "You've got the most beautiful eyes."

"Thank you," I blushed. I was touched by her compliment. Like any girl, getting the mother's approval of a man I deeply cared for mattered to me. I knew she must have wondered if Declan and I were dating. *But no, remember Maíra, you're just friends…*

Late morning hours soon turned into afternoon affairs. There was no time to grieve when phone calls needed to be made, people needed to be comforted and arrangements for a memorial service was also part of a long list of things to do.

But first, Anne was coming by with Declan's niece and nephews, along with some family members of her own. Daisy had already ordered pepperoni and cheese pizza as good distraction for the kids, while Declan mentally prepared himself to ease any potential arguments erupting between his parents and his brother's wife, that is, should they arise. As for me, I just wanted to keep Declan serene. I only had time to quickly jump in the shower and towel dry my hair for a hot second when I heard the doorbell ring.

"Hey mom, Anne and the kids are here," shouted Declan from the living room couch, as his father got up from his recliner to open the front door.

In zig-zag motions, the kids – all younger than five and all with blue eyes like their father John – clamored their way through sofas and floor lamps and up and around the coffee table – and plop! – onto their uncle's lap.

"Come on in!" said Jeremy.

"Hi Maíra, I'm Anne. Nice to —"

Before Anne even had a proper chance to say hello to everyone, including myself, her kids were already making themselves at home and knocking over anything that stood in their way. *Uncle Declan! Uncle Declan!* The excitement and sheer joy on their little faces upon seeing their uncle was contagious.

"Hey buddy! Hey princess!" Declan was equally as thrilled to see them, even as they piled toys on top of toys on top of him. Barbie, Lego, stuffed animals. None of it made any difference when playtime was in order with Uncle Declan.

"Uncle Declan! Look what I got! Can you play this game with me?" shouted his youngest nephew.

"Sure, kiddo. Let me see what you've got here."

I was in disbelief to see how easily his niece and nephews gravitated toward him, almost as if no time had passed at all since they last saw each other. Given Declan's estrangement with his brother, it had been years since the entire family was in the same room together.

And as the kids played, Declan took turns explaining the function of various toys that encompassed most of the entire living room floor. Even if temporarily, the kids were happy here, and it was clear to see why. Declan simply radiated a bright, calming light that made everybody gaze up at him whenever he walked in.

Diiiiiiiiiiiiing. "Pizza is here!" yelled out Daisy, diverting everybody's attention toward her.

For a moment, the kids broke free from Declan's lap to grab greasy slices of pepperoni and cheese pizzas handed out by the adults, only to then rush their way back to him on the couch seconds later. Both his young niece and nephews were talking over their uncle now, sharing stories about their new, favorite Discovery Kid show on TV and recently discovered large-print books at the library. Declan listened intently, while tickling his three-year-old niece's tummy as she let out a high-pitched giggle. I had never seen little kids more in love with their uncle.

And as everyone devoured another slice of pizza, and the adults chattered amongst themselves in the kitchen, it was then that I, too, knew I was falling in love with him.

8

Apartment Prayer

The weekend was coming to a close, yet in a week's time, Declan and I would be back for his brother's service. It was a two-hour drive to my house in South Florida from Melbourne. Since I was without my car, and thus had no way of getting home, Declan insisted on driving me himself, then afterward he would make the nine-hour trek back to Kennesaw.

As we started to load our luggage into the back of his BMW the day after pizza binging, his mother and father gathered outside, waiting for us to approach them and say our temporary goodbyes. Daisy looked slightly calmer now – a soft, rosy glow was restored on her face and the effects of having her oldest son present, and not to mention safe, were enough to release the weighing tension on her shoulders.

"Please call us when you get to Maíra's house," said Jeremy. His arm was now wrapped around his wife, even though she made every discrete effort to push it away.

"No problem, will do," affirmed Declan, raising his hand to slam the door shut to his trunk.

Just before we got on the highway and drove away, I decided now was the time to give Declan my Love-Dare present from the personalized gift store back home. Once we said our final goodbye and closed the driver and passenger doors behind us, I pulled out a ribbon-covered black box, opening it just enough to reveal what lied inside.

"I have a small gift to give you," I said, placing the personalized cross with his name on it in Declan's hands.

"What's this?" he asked.

"I just wanted to get you a little something so that you always know you can turn to your faith, no matter what. It has your name on it and the number of one of our favorite Psalms in the back."

"That's so sweet," he said, as he leaned over to me in the car and gave me a kiss on the lips. A peck of thanks, I summed up in my mind.

By the time we pulled up to my three-building apartment complex, the sun started to set and my father was waiting for me in the parking lot to drop off Lumee, who had stayed with him during my Atlanta-Melbourne adventure. It was the first time my dad and Declan were seeing each other again in more than two years. Not since Declan broke my heart after visiting me in Miami two years ago had they been in each other's presence. It was something I never really discussed with my father afterward. Too painful and bittersweet, I bottled up most of my emotions and learned to deal with them on my own.

"My condolences about your brother. Sorry to see you again under these circumstances," offered my dad, extending his hand to greet Declan, just as were getting out of the car and walking up to the back entrance of my building. He looked refreshed and as if he had gotten a little sun burnt on his most recent morning walk.

"Thank you, sir," replied Declan. It was clear he didn't know whether to address and apologize for my heartache from so long ago, or simply let it be.

When Declan and I first met, he became the only man I introduced my father to who wasn't my boyfriend. "Dad, I think I've met the love of my life!" I joyously shouted one day over the phone. "We're just friends, but you need to meet him. He lives in Georgia but he's coming down to visit in a few weeks. For Memorial Day Weekend." It all seemed like a surreal, distant memory now.

"Please give my condolences to your family as well," said dad, patting Declan on his his shoulders, just as he was getting ready to leave and let us be. "Take care of yourself, Declan. I'll be heading out now so you can guys can have some time to yourselves, alone. I imagine it's been a very rough weekend for you both."

Lumee softly began to cry, hoping my dad would stay. But after a few minutes of giving his four-legged grandson a nice squeeze goodbye, dad got inside his car, and Declan and I made our way inside my apartment. It was Declan's first time visiting my place in Broward. All he had known up to that point was my tiny efficiency in Miami that I used to call home.

I made sure to clean up my apartment just a few days before. There was no trash sitting by the front door, no bra hanging over my bathroom sink, no food containers by the living room TV, no notebooks scattered across my bed and no pee pee pads in a perfect line down the hallway.

"What a nice little place you have here. I like how you've really made it your own," he said, observing these new surroundings for the first time. To his far right stood an *I Kiss Better Than I Cook* sign in my kitchen; and to his left, a personalized painting from when I lived in London as a child hanged on a weathered white wall.

After giving Declan a mini tour of my apartment, we sat across from each other on my couch. Shoes off, feet up. Declan looked at the cross chain I gave him, which was now hanging over his neck and dangling off another one of his Minions shirt.

"You know, Maíra, even with everything that has happened with me, I'm trying to do my best to just put it all in God's hands. Even when it comes down to the celibacy promise I made myself."

"I've been meaning to ask you, how have you been feeling about that lately?" I asked. Lumee had took it to venture off to my bedroom to find a resting spot away from all the hustle and bustle of adult talk, while a part of me wondered if Declan still felt adamant about going a full year without sex. Or maybe, just maybe, his frame of mind had shifted a little.

"I'm still going to stick with it. A full year. I can't even think about sex right now. It's too much. I'm just trying to trust God to lead the way. I made so many bad decisions before, but now I have to let Him show me what is best for me. Which by the way. Let me just say. Sometimes I don't know what I did to deserve you. If it wasn't for you or God, I don't know where I'd be right now."

I wasn't exactly happy with the fact that Declan was still choosing to be celibate for a year, but seeing him be so open and honest, even in a time of such tremendous grief, was humbling to me. I was proud. Proud to see how far he had come since the early days of when we first met. Proud to see him holding on, even when he wasn't sure if there was much of anything left to hold onto anymore.

And I was also a girl who found herself more in awe of him every time we spoke, every time he looked at me, every time he rose to the occasion, and every time he took that leap of faith to learn more about himself and get out of his shell.

Without warning, the realization of it all was something I couldn't have predicted myself and it made tears start to form and trickle down my tired face.

"Aww. What are those tears about? Why are you crying, honey?" he asked, showing concern and scooting himself closer to wipe away my tears. "Is everything okay? Was it something I said?"

"It's nothing. I'm – I'm sorry. I'm a flubbering mess. Give me a minute. I just need to go to the bathroom for a second."

My feelings were overtaking me in a way I never experienced before. I was struggling inside, losing my mind, hating that I couldn't be entirely vulnerable, scared that once the Love-Dare challenge was over, rejection would sit beside me and laugh at my face. I was in the same room as the most beautiful, most amazing man I had ever known, and yet I was all alone. And he didn't even know it.

I excused myself to the bathroom and let myself have a good, quiet cry. I tried to drown out the bubbling sounds by turning on the sink faucet and then flushing the toilet all at once. I couldn't even recognize myself in the mirror. My emerald-green eyes were puffier than a puffer fish, my fine hair was oily to the touch and my chronic rosacea was now in full swing. I couldn't let Declan see me like this. I decided to give it a solid 10 minutes before getting a hold of myself and pasting back on that smile, that smile he was so used to seeing lead the way time and time again.

By the time I re-emerged from the bathroom, my touchup concealer had already softly blended into the pores of my cheekbones and my translucent powder was on thick enough to hide the puffiness around my eyes.

The twinkling evening sky was out in full, panoramic view signaling that it was almost time for Declan to start his long road trip back to Kennesaw.

"Crap! It's getting dark. You're gonna have to leave soon," I sighed, as I tried to keep myself wide eyed, decent-looking (if there was such a thing) and somewhat awake.

"You sure you're okay?" he asked again.

"Yes, I'm fine. I just needed a moment. Thanks for understanding, though. Are you gonna get ready to go soon?"

"In a little bit," he said. "But I wanna stay here with you for a while longer. How about we just take it easy and hang out in your room? Didn't you say you had those Angel Cards to show me?"

I had told Declan during one of our phone conversations that I sometimes turned to a deck of angel cards that were tucked away in my book collection when I needed a moment of clarity, or some answers in my life. Whether it was just for the sake of fun or to get some answers about the future, something about these cards were comforting. So in between playing with my deck of angel cards and doing a mini Tarot Reading of sorts for good measure, I noticed Declan start to relax. And I was starting to do the same too.

"I love doing these relaxing activities," he said, making himself comfortable on my bed, even if my three-layer comfort pillows were out of order. "You're always good at stuff like this. Mind showing me one of your meditation techniques while we're at it?"

"Sure," I responded. "I'd be glad to."

Declan knew that I practiced meditation pretty much all my life, so once he made himself extra comfy by stretching out his legs and laying down on the center of my bed, I began to voice my own set of instructions out loud. At this point Declan had positioned his arms to the side of his waist, letting it fall ever so naturally, as if there was no gravity here to keep them in place. I cleared my throat, and then sat by his feet, waiting until he gave me the cue that he was ready to begin our 15-minute session.

"Okay, I'm ready," he whispered.

"Alright then… let's begin… First… I want you to close your eyes… loosen up your arms… let any thoughts come and go… relax your shoulders… take one deep breath in… one deep breath out… imagine any negative emotion you feel releasing your body… and a bright, white light penetrating you…"

As I began to guide Declan through my personalized meditation exercise, I noticed his face tighten and become flushed. A soft whimper began to cause a light twitch on his lips until it suddenly grew louder and louder, and then, without notice, all I could see were his lips burst open into an uncontrollable sob. Still with his eyes closed, Declan's tears covered his now hard-to-see face.

"Sweetie, what's wrong??!" I asked, stopping the meditation session all at once.

"I'm – I'm just so sorry. I don't know what happened. But as I was listening to you speak, I started to think about Bella," he said, trying to control his emotions against the sounds of his muffled tears. "And the thought of her – of my beautiful daughter – leaves me upset. Because she's so young and yet she's already been through so much. Especially this year after I married that woman. All because of a stupid decision I made. I want her to be happy. I want her to be okay. I want her to forgive me for marrying that woman. *I just love my daughter so much....*"

"Oh, honey..."

With one arm around his shoulder and the other pulling his face close to me, I tried to remind Declan that he was doing everything he possibly could, given the circumstances. For himself. For his family. As well as for his daughter.

"It's going to take some time, but I promise you it's gonna get better. You're gonna get through this, honey. You will."

"I hope so," he said, as he let out a deep breath and sighed.

I could see that in this moment Declan felt like the weight of the world was on him, and everything felt like just too damn much to take on all at once. I felt torn seeing him in such a state of disarray, knowing there wasn't really much of anything I could do for him, except just be there. Hoping my presence alone was enough for a man who was already so strong just on his own.

"I better get going before it gets really dark," remarked Declan, dabbing away his tears with the back of his hand and getting up to search for his car keys nearby.

"Of course. It's been a long day. Let me just put Lumee in the hallway so he doesn't run out the front door, and I'll walk with you to your car."

Even though I knew we would see each other again for John's service in a week, I still struggled to say goodbye to him as we came around the driver seat of his BMW outside. I knew no more words could be spoken between us right now. Because from the two-hour drive to my apartment to our several one-on-one, heart-to-heart talks, it was safe to say we were both emotionally spent.

I was careful not to start crying again when Declan bent down to be at eye level with me and then softly nuzzled his face against my cheek.

"I love you," he whispered, so quietly I could have almost missed hearing it.

"I love you too," I said. "Have a safe drive home, hun. Text me along the way, please."

"I will. I'll text you when I'm pulling over for gas, okay?"

I nodded before waving him goodbye as he drove out into Broward Boulevard, past several intersections and out of my sight.

Once inside my apartment, I curled up in a fetal position on my bed and allowed my crazy, distressing emotions to envelop me completely. Lumee, sensing how upset I was, climbed on top of me in an effort to lick my tears away and ensure mommy everything would be okay. The past few weeks had shaken me to the core and surprised me in unimaginable ways, and I didn't know a damn thing of what I should do about it. I didn't know how much more of the Love Dare I could continue to do, and I didn't if I should stop it all together. After all, we were *just friends.*

10:39 p.m. Journal Entry —

Lord,

I'm writing to you in my journal once more. I'm writing to you because I don't know where else to turn to. We are called to come to you in good times, in bad times and even in moments of uncertainty. As comforted as I am that you are with me, I am also hurting. I am hurting because I have the most incredible man before me, who honors You and is committed to You, but he does not fully see me. He does not recognize how much my heart overflows with love for him. The kind of love that is pure, faithful and true.

He has said that he will no longer make decisions based on what he wants, but rather on what you want for him. Allow him to see and feel the deep love that is tucked away inside his heart, reserved for me. Just as everything I have gone through has led me to him, it has led him to me, too. Please don't let this love I feel for him be in vain. Show him there is no point to seeking false realties when I am his better half.

Let me be the one who encourages him to get out of his comfort zone. Because you put us back into each other's lives for a reason, and I choose to believe we are developing the foundation of a delicate and true love. Reveal that this has been your plan for us every step of the way.

I ask this in Jesus' name. Amen.

9

Half-Drunk and In Love

With both of us huddled up in Declan's living room, Ozzy burrowed his 70-pound limp body next to mine in our same usual spot. While I surfed the Internet and took a sip of hot coffee to unwind, he softly began to snore. The night before, I had flown to Georgia again, and soon, Declan and I would gather everything into his car once more and hit the road for Melbourne – Round Two. His brother's service was only a couple of days away.

Declan had just gotten home from his work shift when he pulled up a chair next to me and began patting Ozzy, who was more interested in watching a squirrel climb up a tree in the enormous back patio.

"Hey, can we have a serious talk?"

A "serious talk" was never something I liked to hear as part of my vocabulary, or anybody else's for that matter. But tough times called for a listening ear, and so I offered mine. "Sure," I reluctantly replied. "Wha'sup?"

"So I've been doing a lot of thinking lately and there are some things I need to say to you."

"Okay… go ahead."

"First of all," he began. "I really need to apologize for how I was two years ago. How I just got up and disappeared. I know I put you through so much pain, and I'm really sorry for that, Maíra. You didn't deserve that."

The lines on his forehead appeared strained, like a crunched up piece of paper that couldn't undo itself. He looked at me for a moment, then like a boy grappling with the proper words to say, continued.

"I also need to say this: I don't know if you're still interested in me, but… you are the right person for me. You always have been. Two years ago was just wrong timing. It was just bad timing for us then. You're like my best friend. Everybody I know approves of you, even my mom.

"And you know my mom isn't an easy person to like. She has only ever approved of me dating American or Spanish girls. Not Brazilian girls. But you – you allow me to be myself around you. I don't have to hide. I don't have to pretend. With you, I can just be me."

I had never heard Declan say so much, so candidly and so nervously, all at the same time. And with every word that sprung from his lips – words I thought I'd never hear – time suddenly froze. I didn't know what to say. It felt too good to be true. *Was he admitting his feelings for me, too? Or was this just another way of him trying to be nice and thank me for sticking around?*

"Wow, Declan. I wasn't expecting that," I sighed. By now I had turned off the computer screen in front of me and instead looked directly into his eyes. Those eyes that always found a way to speak to me so well.

"I kind of have to process everything you're saying. I'm not quite sure what to make of it. But I want you to know that you don't have to apologize anymore. What happened in the past is done. I'm over that now and all I want to do is move forward. But… I do have something I'd like to ask if that's okay. When you say it was bad timing then, do you think there can ever be a right time for us?"

"I don't know," he shrugged. I could tell it had been a long time since he ever felt this vulnerable and exposed. "You know I made a promise to myself that I would not be involved with a woman for a year after this divorce fiasco.

And that meant no sex. But I'm letting God show me the way. He is the only one who knows what decisions I should make. Including any decisions that may involve or be about you. But I am sorry for the pain I once caused you. And I needed you to hear that in person."

I couldn't remember the last time I saw Declan open up his heart completely and unabashedly. But it was everything a woman hoped to receive from a man, and I was no exception.

"Okay, thank you. I understand. We don't need to figure anything out now though, okay? I just want you to be okay."

"I am," he said, now getting up from his chair to kiss me on the forehead. "I don't know what it is about you, but you somehow always make everything feel okay."

Rested and refreshed, we got up early the following morning to begin the drive back down to Melbourne for John's service. Just as I had done all the previous times before, I slept in Bella's room then met Declan in his as soon as I heard the loud humming of his brown noise app turned off. The silk curtains in his master bedroom were still drawn and Declan was still opening his eyes and slowly sitting up on his bed when he saw me walk in.

"Good morning, sunshine. Did you sleep okay? Ready for the drive today? I promise I'll stay awake this time and help you take turns behind the wheel."

"Hey, good morning. Sure, let's start heading out in an hour. I'll make us some coffee and then we can hit the road." His hair was a heaping mile of gorgeous mess on top of his head. Uncombed, untamed yet perfect in its own way and he didn't even realize it.

"Do you have any idea how handsome you look even when you wake up? How is that even possible?" I asked.

"Thanks, it's called using the right hair products that are as cheap as they come."

"Ha. Guess so," I chuckled. "You sure are doing something right. Hey, I'm gonna jump into the shower then I'll meet you downstairs when you're ready."

"Can I join you?"

"Aren't you silly," I responded, poking his arm.

"Well, ya know. It's not like I've never seen you naked before," he said, slowly getting out of bed and tickling my stomach. "Remember two years ago."

"Yes, I remember…. But do you remember how you said you're choosing to remain celibate. For a FULL YEAR, I might add."

"Yes, I know what I said. But doesn't mean I can't play around and have some fun, right?"

"It's either one or the other, mista," I joked. "Besides we need to get going, so I'll see you downstairs, okay?"

Less than an hour later, we loaded everything back into Declan's BMW for the weekend – including Ozzy who at this point was just happy to come along for the long ride – and ventured once again to Melbourne.

This time, both Declan's parents and his mother's best friend, Jane, were waiting for us when we arrived. I already knew a little bit about Jane since her daughter, who was just around my age, was known to have a supreme crush on Declan for the longest time. Jane had been Daisy's best friend for more than thirty years now. Back when Daisy was still living in Spain, the two met through mutual friends, and coincidentally both ended up moving to the United States around the same time.

Like other people Declan hadn't seen in a while, Jane had also become more of a stranger to him over the years. A woman not much older than her sixties, with a mix of unmatched gray-and-blonde hair growing from her roots, Jane acted polite yet slightly cautious around me. She, too, had a short stature just like Declan's mother. It was easy to see why the two were friends. From their petite frames to their common Spanish backgrounds, they were like peas in a pod.

"Let's go inside, everybody," said Daisy, who still looked more tired and overwhelmed than ever. "I've prepared us a table of bread and cheese and some wine that we'll all like." I followed Declan, while Jane walked behind us into the kitchen that now appeared more sparkly clean than I had remembered it.

Everybody took their seat at the dining room table as plates of mini hor d'euvres began to go around. I was told Declan's father had taken his regular afternoon nap, so it was just the ladies on one end of the table, and Declan and I on the other, waiting to see who would break the silence. Jane started to fidget with her hair that kept tickling her forehead when she suddenly looked straight at Declan, almost in awe of the man that stood before her.

"You're looking really handsome, Declan," she remarked. "I remember you as always being a cute boy, but to see how handsome you are now as a man. I just can't believe how good looking you've become."

"Thanks," he replied awkwardly.

I felt myself slightly cringe every time she mentioned *good looking*. Of course he was. Declan was the kind of man anybody easily took a liking to – and not a single person seemed to be immune to his ruggedly yet manly good looks. But it seemed like Jane's vocabulary began to fail her, and for a good twenty minutes or so, the *good-looking* man sitting next to me was all she could speak of. It was also clear that Jane didn't expect me to be here with him. Nobody referred to me as his girlfriend, but it quickly became evident I was more than just a friend.

"Let's go for a walk," interrupted Declan mid conversation, nudging me on my waist. "I need to get out of here for a bit. I'm sure you do too."

He could feel my sense of unease and dread. By now, the ladies started to probe him about the kind of woman he wanted, as well as try to get any concrete answers on the true nature of our relationship. The growing inquisitive nature didn't sit well with either of us. And though Declan approached each question like a gentleman, there was one thing that bothered him: Nobody wanted to mind their own business.

"Ay Dios mio," uttered Daisy, sensing her son was getting a little bit too impatient and riled up for her taste. "Be careful with this one sometimes. He has a bit of an anger problem, you know. Always in a bad mood and with a short fuse. Thank goodness for people like you who can deal with him," she said, pointing at me.

Anger problem? Declan never struck me as somebody with an anger problem. As for bad moods, well – who could blame him. He had been through Hell and back lately, but he never let it be an excuse to treat me poorly. At least up to this point he didn't. He needed me during this vulnerable time, and it was my responsibility to be there for him and make sure he was okay.

Ultimately I didn't know what Daisy was talking about. Surely she must have gotten Declan confused with somebody else.

"Jesus, mother. Okay, Let's go, Maíra" he nudged me sternly, while pulling out a clove cigarette and a set of house keys from his back pocket. "We'll be back. But for the love of God don't wait on us, okay."

As soon as we closed his parent's front door and walked out onto his parents' driveway, a heavy sigh of relief released his chest.

"Ugh! There is only so much of that stuff I can take. I can only take all of this in doses, I swear. I'm sorry if they were making you uncomfortable…"

"I know, honey, I know… Don't worry about it, though. I'm alright."

Much like a ghost town, the neighborhood streets surrounding his parents' home looked dead, though it wasn't much of a surprise considering the vast majority of these modernly-designed houses were still under construction. It was unusually hot on this summer afternoon, upward to 90 degrees with humidity on an all-time high. After only a couple of minutes out in the direct sunlight, droplets of sweat were already forming around Declan's eyebrow, and we began walking around the block to escape the heat, with no pre-determined destination in mind.

An abandoned home with duct-tape covered windows sat atop a small hill by an intersection just down the street from his parents' driveway. A neat pile of construction wooden boards were stacked on top of each other — and all around us – clearly as an indication that this home would soon undergo renovation. My *Havainnas* flip-flips began to accumulate dust in and under my toes. Declan lifted me up with his hands on my hips, sat me on top of one of the sturdy boards, then propped himself next to me.

"Did you notice how Jane was eyeing you down like you were my girl-friend?" he asked, lighting his cigarette.

I looked out into the distance, refraining from making eye contact. "Yeah, I kind of did. That was awkward."

"I feel like she – and my mom – have always wanted me to get with her daughter, but I've never been into her. She's also not my type." He took a moment to pause then glance over at me, seeing me observe a line of ants making their way across the dirt on the ground below.

"I don't know why I feel like I can be so open and honest with you and tell you this. You ever see how different I am around others, but how I let my guard down with you? I mean shit, I can't even tell you stuff about how I'm gonna go a year without me having sex and you don't judge me for it. You accept me for me. And you always laugh at my dumb ass 'Deez Nutz' jokes. And you never judge any stupid thing I do. And you – "

He looked at my fine baby hairs blowing in the wind with a pensive stare. "You know what I really want?"

"No, tell me," I said, lifting up my head to return his gaze.

"To be honest with you, I just want to be with someone who accepts me and my daughter. That's all I want."

I wanted to open my mouth and, for once, let it be known that I under-stood him whole-heartedly. That although I had yet to meet Bella, I already felt like I knew her. Connected with her. As I, too, grew up as an only child of divorced parents. As I, too, understood what it's like to have a step-parent you don't think is right for your father. I wanted to grab him, and have him look at me and see that I am the one who's been here all along.

"I'm sure you'll get what you want," I muttered. "You only deserve the best, and somebody who loves you and supports you, just as you love and support Bella."

"Just gotta trust God, right," he said.

"Yes, always."

Ouch! Crap! What the –! *Swat! Swat!*

A swarm of gnats and pesky little flies were suddenly swirling around us, and diving in toward whatever sweet, juicy blood they sensed from a mile away. Which just so happened to be my own. Before I knew it my legs and feet were covered in bites and rashes the sizes of miniature meteors.

"Declan, I'm allergic to mosquitoes and shit," I whined.

"Okay, let's head back." he laughed. "It's gonna get dark soon. Besides, I don't want them to eat you alive!"

We could hear the upbeat sounds of Spanish music fill the air as we walked back inside his parents' fully air-conditioned living room, thankful to be away from a crowd of bugs that followed us up to the front glass doors. Declan's mom and Jane were frolicking in the swimming pool, singing along to songs of their youth, when they spotted us through the screened pool door.

"Hey! You're back! What took you guys so long!" With a wide grin on her face, Daisy got out of the pool and opened the screened door to the kitchen to grab two glasses of wine. "Do you guys want some?" she asked. "These bottles are from Spaaaaiin."

"Count me in. I'm definitely drinking some wine tonight. It's been a long day," remarked Declan, as his mother poured him a tall glass of Merlot, courtesy of *España*.

I was relieved to see Daisy temporarily distracted over the loss of her youngest son. Although I knew she and Declan were only being civil with each other for the sake of pleasantries, as well as to avoid an all-out rift in my presence, I could also feel a mother's pain that I sensed to be sharp and deep.

It took me back to the time when my own mother and I didn't get along. After all, it was only a few months prior to her death that the veil of heart-break and resentment lifted itself with us.

For as long as I can remember, my mother and I weren't the best of friends. When my parents divorced, the cloud of bitterness that came over my mom left me angry and confused. From time to time, it would still manifest itself and parts of me still resented her for it. Much like I imagined Declan resented his mother for his tumultuous and difficult upbringing, too.

With the second bottle of wine cracked open, Declan and I settled in the living room, while his mom and Jane continued to dance out by the swimming pool like they had never missed a beat their whole lives. My body wanted nothing more than to plop down on their navy-finish sofa and take in this moment of carefree bliss, all thanks to this new Merlot that had made our acquaintance. Declan's father joined us now on the sofa, and while they chatted about somewhat newsworthy events of the day, I pulled out my cell phone to text one of my friends, Angie.

"Girrrrlllllll," I wrote in my slightly drunken stupor. "I am so crazyyyy about him. Everybody is having fun right now. But – But – I'm almost certain that's all there is to it." *Insert sad emojis times ten.*

I could see a looming shadow suddenly looming over me as I finished sending my text. In his typical silly fashion, Declan leaned in, trying to get a clear view of my screen. I quickly flipped my phone shut.

"Who are youuu texting?" he asked playfully, already on his third or fourth glass of wine. "You know you don't need to hide anything from me," he smiled. By the soft glow and glazy look in his eyes, I could tell Merlot, courtesy of *España*, was taking full effect.

He probably thinks I'm texting a boy. "I was texting my friend Angie, silly."

"Oh, right," he said. "Her. Now herrrr I like. She's a good friend to you."

I nodded, as he picked up his iPhone. "Are you going to start texting too?" I asked. Before I could even finish my question, a pop-up text notification lit up my phone.

"I love you," it simply read.

My rosy cheeks were now brighter than the red wine stain on my lips. Though I knew Declan and I had both been drinking, it was the first time I felt in the core of my gut that these were no longer loose words uttered by a mere friend. *No, these were words of a tender love blossoming.* Somehow I could feel it and I wondered if he could feel it, too.

"I love you to the moon and back," I texted back.

Soon, Declan's toes found their way to mine in a game of footsie, and as I looked up at him in my tipsy-affectionate state, I was at ease. Everything we endured and continued to overcome together in the past month or so had us now sitting opposite each other, wondering what could become of this. Wondering how in this perfect entanglement of sorts we found each other again; and wondering whether this time, it was okay to take the next step.

Here, in this unspoken silence between us, my heart felt a sense of peace and joy I couldn't begin to articulate. I was sitting next to my soulmate. And this time I didn't want him to go away again, not now or ever. Nothing felt more right than loving this man I couldn't ignore.

A couple of hours later, when the alcohol started to wear off and Declan's sleepy face found itself nesting in between my chest, I heard the music outside slowly fade into complete silence. Yup, it was time to go to bed.

"Let's go to sleep, sweetie. We have to be ready for your brother's service tomorrow," I said, gently curling my fingers through Declan's wavy hair. "It's getting late."

"Okay," he murmured back.

Declan's father was the first one to get up and say goodnight. Declan soon followed, calling out to his mother, then Jane, who was by now also on the sofa with us. He then approached me last down the line of family goodnights.

"Goodnight, hun," he whispered, before kissing me on the lips. It was the first time he kissed me in front of others without a care in the world.

"Goodnight, sweetie."

And just like that, he kept taking my breath away, *again and again and again.*

Just as I approached my guestroom, with Mr. Teddy Bear waiting to see me once more, I felt a quiet voice nudging at me inside. It was persistent yet steady. *You need to reveal a little bit more of yourself, Maira. Remember what the Love Dare tells you to do: Don't be afraid to show your love. Don't be afraid to remind him that your heart is in the right place. It's now or never.*

Half-drunk yet completely in love, I called out to him. "Declan! Declan!"

A stupid grin, almost as big as mine, appeared at my bedroom door.

"Yes, you called me?" he asked. He looked so much taller than me now as I stood in front of him barefoot, with my heels kicked off and aching feet exposed. "Oh, wait – guess what? You're never going to believe this buuuuuut. My mother said it would be okay if I wanted to sleep in this guest room with you, but of course I told her no, not to worry about it." *Aww, shucks. I wish he hadn't said no. I mean, can anybody even deny our chemistry at this point? It's pretty frigging obvious, even to his mother.*

"Ha, that's funny – and not to mention sweet of her. I'm not surprised," I winked.

"I thought it was funny too. You know if I stayed in this room with you, things would just get wild but we both know that can't happen. So anyway. What is it that you wanted to tell me?"

"Oh, right. I did call you over here for a reason," I suddenly remembered. " I—I – I just want you to know that, well…. Fine, let me just say it. I just – I love you so fucking much, Declan. Like, sooooooo much it makes me want to cry." I exasperatedly blurted out, clearly still under the effects of alcohol and not giving a damn about filtering myself any longer.

"Aww. I love you too, honey," he smiled back. "To the moon and back."

10

The Service

Nobody can prepare you for a memorial service, especially one of your own flesh and blood. When my mother passed away, it took me a month before I felt calm and rather composed to put together the best service in her honor. Late on a warm Sunday afternoon that seemed so long ago now, everybody gathered at St. Jude Church in Miami to pay their respects, those from both near and far. But just as I thought I had enough time to collect my thoughts and self-restrain my emotions, the moment I delivered my mom's eulogy turned into one of the hardest moments of my adult life. To this day, I can't remember what I said in her speech. All I remember is that I fumbled through my words and tears soaked through my never-before-used black dress I had picked out for just the occasion.

As strong as everybody knew Declan to be, I also knew attending his brother's memorial celebration would, undoubtedly, have a profound impact on the man who strived to keep it together for everybody around him.

The memorial ceremony took place at a tropical beach on the south side of Melbourne, inside a small banquet hall overlooking the Atlantic Ocean. By the time we arrived early to the ceremony, there were already a few dozen people waiting to pay their respects to John's family, especially to the remaining brother of the beloved man who was no longer with us.

Dressed in my flowery, knee-length black skirt and faux suede heels, I followed Declan and his parents inside and found a seat close to the pictures of John that were on a long table display. His mom kept her sunglasses on when anyone walked up to her, while his dad quietly sat in a corner of the room, not wanting to draw any attention to himself. It was still a hot summer day, but nobody seemed to care about the low-blowing A/C that barely cooled any sweat trickling down our backs.

Almost in an instant, a number of people I had never seen before began approaching Declan as he straightened out his black suit and tie every few seconds or so to ensure he represented the perfect image of a strong older brother. High school classmates that Declan had not run into in more than twenty years joined together to offer their condolences and any other thoughts that conjured inside their heads.

"Oh, you're so handsome."

"John is so missed. He had the most beautiful blue eyes."

"Is this your girlfriend?"

"What have you been up to, man?"

"I remember when you and your brother were always up to something in college."

"John was so smart. Probably the smartest person I've ever met."

"How's life treating you in Georgia? Good to see you in town with the family."

As soon as Anne and her three kids arrived, the energy in the banquet hall turned to such palpable sadness, tears began to build in people's eyes without them even realizing it. One by one, more children began pouring in, and adults looked around to see who they knew and if this composed and confident man greeting everybody was, in fact, John's brother.

Before the commencement of the service, I took a moment to excuse myself and go to the bathroom. Anne was by herself there, standing in front of a full-length mirror, with her straight ashy-blonde hair in a low pony tail and a beautiful summer dress that sashayed along with her.

Seeing me walk in, she tugged on my arm, and looked up at me with a soft smile. "I'm so glad you're here, Maíra. Here for not just me but for Declan, too. I may not know you well, but I can tell already that you have a huge heart."

I didn't know what to stay. I still couldn't understand how so many of Declan's loved ones were displaying gratitude toward me when I should be the one thanking them.

"It's an honor to be here, Anne. Thank you for allowing me to be here in remembrance of John."

"How are you doing?"

"I'm okay – you know, trying to be strong for the kids. I think I'm no longer in shock about everything but it still hurts. There are times I miss him so much."

"I completely understand," I said, as I offered to put my arm around her. "You let me know if there's anything I can do for you, anything at all. Can I walk you back out to the room for the service?"

"That would be nice, thank you."

I wondered how Anne, Declan and the rest of his family could find the strength to keep it together when the world didn't seem to be by their side. But then I remembered that grief wasn't nice to anyone, so the only way to get through it sometimes meant getting through it with the help of others.

Back in my still vacant seat, I saw the pastor enter the room and move toward the front row of onlookers, as he got ready to lead service. Coincidentally, Pastor Mark was somebody Declan went to high school with, years ago when he still lived in Florida. Everybody seemed to take their proper seats now, but before speaking to the gathered crowd, Mark took some time to go around the room and introduce himself to each guest.

"Thank you for being here to celebrate John's life," he would say every time he approached someone to shake their hand, even if it was somebody that could have just walked in from the streets for all he knew. There was a quiet grace about him and a warm smile that made you feel surprisingly comforted.

Then, as the room started to get unmistakably quiet, it became time for the service to begin.

While dozens more family members and friends found their seats, and children were hushed or cradled to not make a sound, Mark began to ask those in the room to share memories of John while he, too, added some of his own. There were some who laughed recalling clever, funny pranks John got away with in high school, and then there were others who spoke of regret that they lost touch with the man who was as silly as he was generous with friends.

When it was the pastor's turn to approach the podium, he thanked everyone for taking some time out of their day to remember "John, a loving father." Anne echoed that sentiment when she delivered her own speech, also sharing that she knew she was "in trouble" the moment she laid eyes on her future husband.

"He had these gorgeous blue eyes I couldn't turn away from. I just knew I had to get to know him," she said.

In between tears, everybody smiled and chuckled. It was as if we had all been there at one point or another in time. But it was only when Declan got up to speak and share memories of his younger days with his brother that everybody rushed for their tissues and not a dry eye was left in the room.

Nervously approaching the podium, Declan pulled out a small sheet of paper only to a second later crumple it back inside his pocket. He quickly realized he didn't need a piece of paper to put his emotions into words. So as he rubbed his sweaty palms against the side of his black jacket and lifted his eyes up to speak, every single pair of eyes were on him at the podium.

"First of all, I want to thank all of you for being here. I've seen many similar faces and also some I had not seen in a while. I'm sorry we had to reunite under these circumstances," he began.

"Like for so many here, my brother was a big part of my life. We had a lot of fun growing up together. As kids, you can say we were kind of tied to the hip. We were only 18 months apart so it was the natural thing to do. But in many ways being so close in age also meant we were often up to no good. There were many times we ran across the—"

He stopped for a second, his eyes now lowered, avoiding contact with anyone in the room. "I can't do this – I'm sorry – I can't go on. I just can't deny that I'm so angry at him. I'm so fucking mad! Why! Why in the world did you have to go, John! Why aren't you still here? I can't even understand my emotions right now. You should still be here, dammit!"

Declan's voice cracked as he fought in vain to continue. I had never seen him speak so bravely and candidly in public. It was absolutely gut-wrenching to see. Because even as he tried to keep loved ones together, while simultaneously taking care of his own problems, here was a man in immense pain. The family's remaining son was suddenly holding the weight of the world on his shoulders, and it was a burden he was bound to soon fall under.

Day 21: Love is honorable. Do something today that shows you honor and respect the person you love.

After the conclusion of the service, while everybody seemed to hug each other tightly one last time before walking to their respective cars, close family members and friends were invited to stick around a little longer and spread John's ashes into the sea. Declan was one of the first to lead the crowd that included his parents, a couple of his closest friends from college, Anne and her family, and Jane and myself. Declan's young niece and nephews also followed behind him to the beachfront, giggling as they threw sand on his back then innocently ran away before he had a second to catch the sandy culprit.

Then, while everybody gathered in a circle by the water and offered a few prayers to the crystal-blue skies, Declan walked the opposite direction alone, toward low-lying crashing waves that swept inches away from his feet. And in a moment of solidarity, he opened himself up to the sea.

I could see him from a distance, his neck-length dark hair slicked back, and his suit and tie snug around his frame. His eyes, cast on the horizon, were at peace here. "I've always loved the beach," he would often say to me. And here, it seemed, at least for right now, he could let go and release.

He had done in Melbourne what he set out to do. He had carried his family through the gripping motions of grief – and now; he was ready to return home.

11

The Ride Home

With my regular work shift and a million editorial assignments waiting for me the next day, I drove back home to South Florida immediately following the ceremonial spreading of John's ashes. I promised Declan I would text him as soon as I got home.

"Alright. I'll be waiting for your text. Drive safe, okay?" he said, before walking me to my car at the closing of his brother's service and giving me a kiss goodbye.

I was still trying to wrap my brain around everything that had transpired over the weekend. It was a combination of trying to maintain my composure around Declan and his family, while still trying to hide my feelings from everyone around me. I still couldn't let anybody know or see what I was feeling for Declan, especially during these delicate times that required me to simply be supportive and extend a helping hand to my grief-stricken friend.

The last thing I wanted Declan to deal with was my own emotions that I continued to struggle with and understand and make sense of myself. But my feelings were growing by the day. Not only were they growing faster than flowers seeing the light of day for the first time in the spring, these feelings were now every bit a part of me.

The magnitude of everything that had happened these past two weeks finally caught up to me as I began driving down the Florida Turnpike, with a good couple of hours still to go before I got home. But instead of speeding away and cursing the gods for striking me with Cupid's arrow, I decided I needed a moment. I needed to take a moment for myself and remember to well, breathe.

Catching a glimpse of a gas station right off a nearby exit, I parked my car in a hidden parking space where nobody could see me, then lowered my head into the palm of my hands and let a puddle of tears unexpectedly wash over me. Here, I didn't have to be afraid to cry. I had never felt so in love, yet there was also nothing that terrified me more.

The Love-Dare challenge was still under wraps. I still had the proper friend persona down pat. By Day 21, I made sure to give Declan a number of gifts, ranging from a collection of Minion stickers to a beachy photo frame, to take home with him to Georgia; all part of a full week of dares that coincided with words of encouragement or daily compliments I was also instructed to act upon according to the challenge.

And just as I was seeing to it that Declan did not have to face any of these hard times alone, inside, I found myself breaking into a million pieces. All because he still didn't know about my feelings, and I was scared that the day he'd look me in the eyes and tell me we couldn't be anything more than friends was rapidly approaching. Love is blind, they say, yet I simply couldn't see past the callings of my own heart.

Nine more days of Love Dare, I kept repeating to myself. Nine more days.

After blotting my face with a cleansing wipe from my glove compartment and dabbing away any remaining streaks of mascara, I turned the ignition back on and resumed my two-hour drive home. But I needed to talk to some-one – anyone – and get these feelings off my chest. Naturally I decided to call my friend Angie.

Angie was more than a friend to me. We had known each other for a couple of years, and though she lived in Brazil now, I felt closer to her more than I did with several of my geographically local friends. If there was such a thing as a heart of gold, hers was overflowing with buckets of blessings and treasures. She was the kind of person you simply wanted by your side.

"Hi, Angie. It's me," I said when she picked up the phone after the first ring. "I've been dying to talk to you – you have no idea. I don't even know where to begin telling you about the last couple of days. I just left John's service and –"

"What's going on, sweetheart?" she calmly asked. "You don't sound too okay." I could hide from everybody else and the world, but not Angie. She could always see right through me when something was bothering me. It was if she had radar that picked up on my brainwaves and heart pangs even thousands of miles away.

"Oh, Angie, I can't keep this to myself any longer. I'm falling for Declan hard and I don't know what the hell to do about it. And to think I still have nine days of this miserable Love-Dare challenge to complete. I'm scared it will all be in vain in the end."

"Don't say that. Everything's going to be okay. You're following your heart, and I'm sure by now Declan feels your love for him. Remember, he chose YOU to be with him during all of this. He choose YOU to drive down with him to Melbourne. That's not all for nothing."

"I know, but what if he is only turning to me because he feels safe enough to now consider me one of his closest friends? What if I'm reading into his words and recent gestures of affection a little too much?" I cried. At this point I had to pull over again before risking getting into an accident, all in the name of heartache.

"Sweetheart, he wouldn't want you to go to the end of the world and back with him if he didn't feel something for you, too. I have a feeling you will soon be more than pleasantly surprised once you reveal the Love-Dare. And you have to also remember, there's a reason he choose you to be the woman to help him through the hardest times of his life."

"I sure wish you were here, my friend."

"I wish I was there too, but you've got this. Believe in yourself and believe in your love for Declan. Let me know when you've made it back to your place, okay?"

Three hours had passed by the time I finally pulled up to my parking spot and walked into my apartment, with only my house keys and cell phone with me. I was tired and worn out from all the crying. Bringing my carry-on luggage inside could wait until the next day.

Too lazy to even remove my contact lenses, I went straight to bed without even turning on my bedroom light. But when my phone kept vibrating and wouldn't let me be still, I noticed a couple of unanswered calls from Declan, along with a few urgent text messages I apparently missed.

"Did you make it home?"

"Are you okay?"

"Maíra? You there?"

"Maíra, answer me please."

I wasn't in the mood to talk. I knew that if I picked up my phone and called him back, Declan would see that I was upset, and he would be clueless as to why, and I wasn't about to tell him. But after a minute or two, I called him back anyway. This wasn't the time to start playing games.

"Hey, I'm here. I just got home."

"Wow. That was a long drive. Took you much longer than I expected. Weren't you supposed to get home an hour ago? Did you run into some traffic or was there an accident?"

"Yeah, there was quite a bit of traffic," I fibbed.

"Oh, okay. I'm glad you're home now. I was starting to get worried, hun. Hey, listen. I know it's been a rather long day – for the both of us – but I wanted to thank you for everything you've done for me and my family. They appreciate it. And I appreciate it too. Thank you for being there for me. Even if you did see me see me break into pieces at my brother's eulogy. But then again, you've seen so much of me already."

"Of course. That's what friends are for. I was so proud of you today, the way you handled everything. I really was. You doing okay?"

"I'm fine, I guess."

"Sounds like you could use some good company with your family. Do you wish you were around others?"

"Not others. Just you."

With less than two weeks away until Declan's birthday, I was determined to follow through with everything the Love-Dare challenge required me to do. I still had much to jot down and capture in the scrapbook that was now coming together so nicely. There wasn't a single day I had not completed any of the dares outlined in the challenge, and though sometimes I felt emotionally drained, I was too far in now to let it all go.

Not too long after, I booked another flight to visit Declan in Georgia, this time for his birthday. The month of August was upon us now, and I hoped it would provide the both of us a much-needed breather after the unfortunate circumstances of experiencing tragedy after tragedy. His second divorce was finalized by now, and his brother was now also finally resting in peace. Soon, everything else would be revealed.

PART III –

When We Met

*"Important encounters are planned by the
souls long before the bodies see each other."*

— Paulo Coelho

12

Kennesaw

On the cusp of my thirties, I fancied my way around the dating field so many times I could barely keep track of the multitude of random numbers on my cell phone. There were plenty of bountiful nights where the type of alcohol I drank did not matter, as long as I had a beer or shot (preferably vodka or tequila) to cha-ching to. Time and time again, I hit the nightlife scene with my black heels leading the way and my all-natural lip balm ready to pucker up the first charming guy who approached me. If there was a trophy for who could attain the most meaningless dates, I was the champion. But the truth is, I was mentally and emotionally at a crossroad, feeling empty and alone, just like the bottle of vodka I put away night after night.

Nobody I met was of my caliber. More than a year had passed since my last long-term relationship ended, and stupid chit-chat with strangers that consisted of elementary English proved to be so futile, I would have preferred to stare at the wall. This was not the life I envisioned for myself. There had to be somebody who would "get" me, as I would him.

Though I had been fortunate enough to experience love before – first with somebody I was engaged to in my early twenties, followed by a five-year relationship with a Mexican man – I wanted to finally meet the love of my life, once and for all. I didn't care about how perfect a guy's hair looked, or whether or not he could hook it up at a fancy, five-star restaurant. I wanted somebody of substance, somebody who would make me feel alive, whatever that meant. *It had been too long.*

I was living in my tiny Miami efficiency when I pondered on these thoughts one night while home alone. I had just returned from another pitiful date with your typical average-looking guy who insisted on maintaining a consistent dialogue with his vehicle's GPS, more than he did with me.

"Go straight ahead and make a right at the light. Then make an immediate left at the intersection."

"Okay, got it. Make a right then a left. Thank you, Suri," he would respond back to his imaginary friend.

I refused to believe that my life was now reduced to dates with people who cared more about answering a silly robot than they did me. Discouraged, I surrendered to the only thing I knew could help me and got on my knees to pray. My heart felt heavy from all the disappointments of short-lived romances and half-assed prospects that led to nowhere. Something just had to give. So closing my eyes, I started to voice everything I had been feeling for a long time out loud.

"Lord," I began, "It's been so long since I felt like there was somebody I could talk to, somebody I could connect with. It seems like my days are passing me by and I'm stuck. I'm stuck in a haze of meeting endless guys who are no good for me. Guys who are ultimately a waste of my time. And I want it stop.

"But I need you to please help me. Will you bring me the person that is right for me? I promise you that I will not care about his past, or any baggage he might carry. I will not judge anything he has been through. I will put all of that aside, as long as he is a good man. I'm done surrounding myself with boys. I just want to be with the man who is truly right for me and my heart. If it is Your will, can you provide me the answer to my prayer?"

A month later, I met Declan.

As fate would have it, Declan and I found each other online, which had by now become commonplace in the world of modern-day dating. Or rather, to put it more appropriately, I found him. It was a random Friday afternoon when I stumbled upon his profile in my match results, while checking out a popular dating website I tended to browse through whenever boredom seemed to get the best of me.

With an 89 percent match between us, he easily stood out from all the other men who only cared about posting shirtless pictures of themselves and two-word answers in their "About Me" section. As I began to fumble through this stranger's profile, I became drawn to his lively personality and laughed at the witty descriptions used to describe himself. Plus, it helped that he was easy on the eyes, too.

He seemed like the right fit – that is, until I noticed the location listed on the far-right corner: "Kennesaw, GA." *Georgia? What the hell? Why in the world would this dating website match me with somebody outside my state? Did I read that correctly? Everybody else is in Florida. Surely, this must have been a mistake.*

I contemplated for a minute or two whether or not I should message this 39-year-old man whose name I soon discovered was Declan. Captivated by his profile, I found myself giggling every time I gave his page another run through. I wanted to keep reading more about this charming and funny person on the other side of the screen. And although I couldn't pin-point it exactly, something else about him made me feel like maybe we could easily hit it off.

Oh, what the hell. Just do it, Maira.

Before I had a second to change my mind, I typed out a quick email and hit send. Within minutes, my computer screen flashed with a response.

That first night, Declan and I spoke for hours on end, just getting to know each other. Soon it was clear we had way more in common than we could have ever thought. From sharing some of our favorite songs (to my surprise he was also into Christian music), to reflecting on experiences of our past, our conversations seemed easy, instant and effortless.

Divorced for a year, I soon learned that Declan had a pre-teen daughter from his 10-year marriage with his then only ex-wife. Bella was her name, and she, too, lived life as an only child. I could sense Declan's face light up every time he spoke of his daughter, even as he mentioned her to me, a person he had never met. Their relationship reminded me so much of my own with my father. They were close to the hip, and there was nothing in the world he wouldn't do for his blue-eyed princess. In every sense of the word, she was daddy's little girl, and he was her fierce and loyal protector.

The mood took a detour from such happy and joyful topics when the conversation turned to the rest of his family. Not one to shy away from the difficulties of his life, Declan had no problem admitting that he was estranged from most of his family members, including his mother and brother, whom he hadn't seen in a while. They both lived close to Canova Beach Park in Melbourne, Florida. Declan was the only one in his family to leave the Sunshine State after he received a job opportunity in his early twenties that he couldn't pass up. And while they initially stayed in touch, family strains and unresolved conflict eventually got in the way.

I could particularly relate to the difficulties that Declan often experienced with his mom – from the Victim Card she would throw in his face, to the emotional and mental abuse he endured behind closed doors. A child should never have to see their mother taken away to a psychiatric ward but Declan did, and much of his upbringing affected him still, to greater capacities that I would only realize later.

When it came to his brother John, Declan knew to keep a distance. Although they were buddy-buddies in college, John soon started exhibiting symptoms of mental illness. Which ultimately took a drastic toll on the entire family. So as far as Declan was concerned, it was just him and Bella in his world, and that was good enough for him.

There was so much passion in Declan's voice every time he spoke. And he was clearly unashamed to talk about his struggles along the way, whether it revealed his mishaps with drugs in the past or the mental illness stigma that continued to plague his family. I barely knew him still, but within the first few hours of talking, I was already drawn to Declan's beautiful, quiet strength.

The more we spoke, the more comfortable I felt sharing some of my own challenges growing up. I told him about my own childhood and the cultural adjustments I faced every time my parents and I moved to a new city or continent. By the time I was 11, we had already lived in four different countries. Since Declan was a military baby, he, too, grew up in more places than he could keep count. Including Florida, where we both coincidentally attended high school just a couple of hours away from each other.

From the beginning, I could tell that Declan and I were more similar than we were different. Our backgrounds were almost identical, and even though in many ways life had given us different cards to play, we were still buckling up and bracing ourselves for the ride.

As a way of not taking life so seriously, it was comforting to realize that we also shared the same sense of humor. Declan was more random and sarcastic than anybody I had ever met, including myself, and I loved hearing his stupid jokes he got a good kick out of, even when they made no sense to anybody else but himself.

"I must warn you, I can be very sarcastic," he said that first night we spoke. We were still talking each other's ear off on the phone, and by now our topics of conversation gave way to us being in a silly mood.

"Ha! Not to worry, I'm the same way. It's all good."

"Alright then. That's a relief," he smiled. "So what did you have for dinner tonight?"

"Chicken with some rice. Boring, I know. But sometimes you just have to grab whatever leftovers you have, know what I mean. What about you?"

"Deez Nutz!" he randomly chuckled before taking a few seconds to compose himself. "Okay, sorry. Shoot. Did I cross the line with that one?"

"Hmm. Let me think. Nope! Not if I can grab Deez Nutz with you!" I playfully countered, trying to amuse him.

"Ha ha! Good one! I think I like you. You can be a nerd just like me." Yup, nerdy and goofy, we were both like two peas in a pod.

Before long, the sounds of our voices slowly began to trail off in the distance as we started to get tired. The time on my cell phone indicated it was two o'clock in the morning, and thus time for us to go to bed. But neither of us wanted to call it a night. After all, our conversations had come so naturally, so seamlessly, we could have stayed up for hours talking about anything and everything in between. But this was just the beginning of a blossoming friendship with a complete stranger who made me feel certain that, in the days and weeks to come, we would have plenty to talk about, and plenty of ways to get to know each other still.

"Gosh. Have you noticed how long we've been talking?" I asked, while trying to cover the loud moaning sounds of my sixth consecutive yawn. "Almost six hours straight. Isn't that cray cray! Maybe we should go to bed, mista. How about I talk to you tomorrow?"

"Sure thing," he responded, "We can talk more then."

"Okay, sounds like a plan. Goodnight, Dec—"

"Actually, wait," he said, interrupting me. "Can I tell you something, Maíra? This may sound a bit crazy and all since I know we just started talking tonight, but it's weird. I feel like I've known you forever. There's something about you. You just amaze me... Sorry if that is a bit too forward, but I guess you've already seen how random I can be."

"No worries, it's one of the things that already draws me to you. There's something amazing about you too, Declan. I mean that. I'll talk to you tomorrow, okay? Pleasant dreams."

Over the course of the following days, I looked forward to the moments my phone rang with an incoming call from Declan. Or when I got home and saw a Skype notification on my opened laptop for us to video chat. In an instant – without any sure-fire explanation as to why – I found myself wanting to talk to him, not just for bit here and there as a means of distraction or good company, but all the time. And the more we took the time getting to know each other, the clearer it became to me that for some odd or unknown reason, we were simply destined to meet. Even if we were hundreds of miles apart.

Months prior to meeting Declan online, I purchased a pair of tickets for my best friend Oceana and I to attend one of the most popular self-help book conferences coming to town. Which was just so appropriately titled the "You Can Do It!" workshop, and with good reason. The likes of Dr. Wayne Dyer, Louise Hay and Brian Weiss were scheduled to lead to the delight of thousands of South Florida locals who were willing to pay an arm and a leg to be in the presence of one of these New Age greats. Declan and I had only been talking for a full week when the long-awaited day of the conference finally arrived.

Bright and early on a Saturday morning, Oceana called me to let me know she was on the way to the Fort Lauderdale Convention Center that was fully equipped to accommodate thousands of unfamiliar faces of people who wanted to conquer the world, one goal at a time. Or something like that. In reality, everyone was simply eager to reclaim control of their emotional health by listening to a bunch of so-called inspirational experts tell us how we needed to change our lives. And boy, were we ready.

After we agreed to meet at the front entrance of the convention center, Oceana and I scurried our way to an already crowded lobby floor, mostly full of women gleefully rummaging to buy a collection of self-help books at any of the merchandise stands, just as Dr. Wayne Dyer prepared to take center stage as the first speaker of the day.

With two empty chairs available in the back row of the auditorium in the lobby, Oceana and I took our seats, sipping a bland cup of coffee from the lobby, as we waited for talks of the importance of living a happy and fulfilled life to begin.

I could feel a buzzing vibration going off inside my purse when I noticed Declan texting me. It was so early still, only 8 a.m. *Did something happen?*

"Maíra, I can't sleep. I just want you to know that I already miss talking to you. You remind me of the sun rising. Call me crazy, but I wish you were here."

His sweet, romantic gesture was enough to make me smile. I'll text him later I thought. But just as I was about to put my cell phone away, it flashed again with another message.

"Okay, soooo. Now you're really gonna think I'm crazy, but just hear me out for a second. Would you be willing to fly up here today or tomorrow for a few days? I know we only started talking a week ago, but I would love to see you. And oh, no worries about the plane ticket. I'll pay. Consider it my treat."

Surely somebody else had texted me by mistake. I double checked my phone. Nope, it was Declan alright.

"Are you serious?" I pressed on. "For real or are you playing?"

"For real."

Laughing, but trying to keep it to a minimum as to not disturb others around me, who were by now fully entranced by Dr. Wayne Dyer's speech, I texted him back. "What brought this about?"

"I don't want to wait weeks to see you. That's all."

I didn't know whether to think something had happened overnight that caused Declan to lose his damn mind, or if he was just taking the liberties to be open and expressive with me. Either way I couldn't deny how badly I wanted to see him, too. So I did what any girl in my shoes would do: I turned to my best friend to help me snap out of it and tell me how this boy was clearly bat-shit crazy.

"Girl, you're never going to believe this," I began rambling out loud. "Look at this text! Declan wants me to fly up to see him, like tomorrow, out of nowhere, fly up to see him! What the fuck am I to do?! Should I go? Oh my god. No, wait, I can't. Who would take care of Lumee? And my dad! Nobody can tell my dad! As a matter of fact, I can't tell anyone about this! Right. Right??"

"Maíra!" she interrupted me, quickly pulling me out of the auditorium before everybody eyed us down with their evil stares. "Listen, first of all, it's too cute to see you freak out like this. Second, here's the deal: You're always telling others to live life to the fullest, right? To take chances and wear their hearts on their sleeves. But guess what."

"I don't know what," I said, clearly in a sudden state of frenzy. "That's why I'm talking to you!"

"Okay, so you want my advice. I'll tell you what then. It's time you start taking your own advice. Go see him! DO IT!"

"What did you just say?"

"You heard me. I said go see him! Maíra, I may not know much about this guy, but I know you. And I know how your face lights up whenever you talk about him. He definitely doesn't sound like other guys you've met. Besides, life is short. I'm sure you won't regret it."

"Are you sure? Do you really think it's okay for me to go? What about Lumee? What about –"

"Don't worry about Lumee. Stay at my house tonight and I'll drop you off at the airport first thing in the morning. I'll make sure Lumee is taken care of. Remember, you only live once."

And so less than 12 hours later, I found myself on a plane to Kennesaw, Georgia; while happily or foolishly taking my best friend's advice. Not knowing whether I was making a big mistake, or one of the best decisions of my life.

"Are you nervous yet?"

"Hush you!" I playfully fired back at Declan's text message.

It was April 27th, 2014. Only hours earlier, I listened to Dr. Wayne Dyer tell a room full of people how the best life requires us to take chances, and now, here I was, putting his words to the test. While still not quite knowing what I was doing, I strolled down the never-ending maze of the Atlanta Hartsfield-Jackson International Airport for the first time mere moments after my flight landed.

"Remember to take the train down to Terminal 2, then go south, then make your second left. Keep going until you're outside. I'll meet you by the parking lot," read another text from Declan. *How the fuck was I supposed to know which way south was?*

Stepping out into the Arrivals parking garage on the second floor, I instantly saw him. Maybe it was his height. At 5'11, Declan could be seen from half a mile away. Or maybe it was his smile. Warm and inviting like fresh bedsheets after finishing laundry.

I could imagine the size of Declan's charming grin when we spoke over the phone, and in person, it was the exact personification of what I pictured in my head. Seeing him for the first time, my lips opened up to a smile wider than the grin on his face.

His silky-soft brown hair, perfectly trimmed on the sides of his neck, could have been the envy of every LA hairstylist. It was thick and full, and tempting enough to run my fingers through. Sensually at first then all at once.

Declan also had the muscular build of a man who took pride in taking care of himself, yet was equally as comfortable throwing on his favorite Minions t-shirt. And, of course, he was simply *handsome*. The kind you expect to see on the cover of a GQ magazine minus the arrogant flair and overdone airbrush tanning. It faded everything else around you, and had you convinced you were led to this moment, and that something or someone was on your side. *Oh, how those online pictures don't do him justice.*

I wanted to take a mental image of him and freeze it in a picture frame. I wanted to take his dreamy eyes and put them on my bedside to wake up next to every day. I wanted to learn everything about him and then nothing at all.

"Hey there! You're here!" Declan spotted me looking straight at him, causing me to quickly break my stare.

"Hey! How's it going? So we finally meet huh," I said, bashfully looking up at him. "I still can't believe I'm here!"

Those initial moments around Declan made everything spin around me. Like a silly school girl who doesn't know what to do around her crush, I clammed up. The nervous jitters started to take hold and my fingers trembled in the side pocket of my jacket.

"I know, right. About damn time!" he said. "My car is right down this way."

Pulling onto the strap of my expandable carry-on bag, Declan and I walked up to his BMW parked in front of the parking garage meter. The BMW was one of the few possessions he kept after the finalization of his divorce from Bella's mom. Married for a decade, separated for just under a year, their custody agreement was now effectively in full swing. Time was divided equally with each parent, and for an adoring father who saw his daughter every single day, this was not the easiest of things to adjust to.

My visit took place during a weekend when Bella was with her mom. She was only nine then. While Oceana helped me pack items for my trip the night before, Declan called me to tell me about everything he had lined up for our four-day itinerary of "let's just have some fun."

Kennesaw was roughly 30 or so minutes outside of Atlanta. As Declan and I began to drive away and pull out of the airport, he put his hand on my lap, and asked me if I wanted to grab a bite to eat before we headed to mid-day church service in a neighborhood called Buckhead.

"Sure, I could do Denny's or something like that, if you don't mind."

"We don't really have Denny's here, honey," he laughed. "But I'll tell you what we do have: Cracker Barrel. Ever heard of that?"

"I have actually! But we don't have one in Miami, so I've only been during road trips to Orlando."

"Well then, today might just be your lucky day!"

I wondered what crossed his mind every time he looked at me and smiled. I still couldn't believe that I was standing before the man who somehow convinced me to fly up to see him last minute. But there was no fighting against something that just felt right. Even if I still didn't know how or why.

Attending service at Buckhead Church was next on the list, followed by a hike at Kennesaw Mountain National Battlefield Park. I had a personal wish to see a deer. Living in South Florida, squirrels and lizards were the extent of wildlife as I knew it. I hoped and prayed a docile, little deer would approach us up the mountain and smile at its new guest. *Okay, maybe I watched too much Bambi as a child.*

As we began our trek up the mountain, we heard a loud rumble while a sudden downpour of heavy rain and dark clouds hovered over us. No umbrella. No plastic bags. We were suddenly running for our lives – or rather the nearest shelter we could find. I waited by a public bathroom as Declan pulled up in his car, and in a matter of minutes, we were home.

His house was much larger than what I could have ever imagined. A lavish Georgia mansion of sorts. Three empty rooms – one with an electric fireplace – completed the layout downstairs, while three additional bedrooms circled around the top of a long-winded staircase that could give you all the exercise you needed for one day.

While Declan showed me around, I could see a few toys peeking out of a playroom that appeared to be of Bella's. She was a fan of stuffed animals and all things pink as far as I could tell. Still soaking wet, I wrapped myself around a clean, fresh towel Declan grabbed from his garage and dried my feet on an entrance mat by the front door. I needed to change my clothes before

I embarrassed myself even further, but before I could excuse myself, Declan stopped me.

"Here, come with me," he motioned, reaching out his hand and leading me up the stairs of his two-story suburban house. "You'll be staying in my room while I sleep in Bella's. I made sure to have everything you may need in here. Toiletries, shampoo, conditioner, toothpaste – you name it. If there's anything I'm missing, just let me know."

I felt bad that Declan was giving up his room for me when I could have easily slept on the couch. But as if reading my mind, he insisted, "Really. It's no problem at all. You'll sleep better in my bed anyway. The mattress is memory foam."

I could only half-awkwardly smile at him and nod my head in gratitude.

After changing into a dry pair of dark jeans, I met Declan back downstairs in the sitting room across his living room. A fireplace with artificial coals and a soft shadow behind it graced us in the center. *Ooh, what a pretty fireplace. Now that's something you don't see back home.* I stretched out my tired legs on his overstuffed, leather couch, already making myself at home, and put on a pair of oversized men's socks he handed me a few minutes before. Finding a spot next to me, Declan sat down and comfortably curled up his legs over mine.

"Well, that hike was an adventure!" he remarked, combing a long strand of still wet hair out of his face. "How are you feeling?"

"Right! That was so much fun, though! Thank you for taking me there. I'm good. You know, just a little wet – but good."

"Wet huh," he joked.

"You dork. You know what I mean," I grinned back, throwing one of the fluffy sofa cushions directly on his chest.

There was no need for an icebreaker anymore. Engrossed in our conversations, I felt safe, allowing everyday worries of my life back in South Florida to fade away, just as I imagined he could do the same around me. And there was something about the twinkle in Declan's eyes that turned to a soft hazel when it looked at mine that told me I could find a piece of home here in his presence. Because here in his presence nothing could trouble me.

Previous days of talking on the phone and texting each other back and forth could not compare to these moments in person where Declan gave me room to know the smallest and most intimate parts of him.

I knew he was a wild child in college. I knew he was the popular jock in school. I knew he was obsessed with all-things Minion. I knew his stupid jokes. I knew he slept late. I knew he didn't like Rose wine. I knew he had seen spirits before. I knew he was studying to be a child psychologist. I knew he was a clean freak.

Sitting close to him now, I also knew his vulnerable side.

I knew he didn't exactly have the perfect upbringing. I knew he was estranged from most of his immediate family. I knew how much he absolutely loved his one and only daughter. I knew how much he missed her when she wasn't around. I knew when he was putting up a front with others. I knew he suffered from depression. I knew he was experiencing a mid-life crisis of sorts approaching his forties. I knew when he was hurting, and I knew the reasons behind the unsettling anguish that sometimes made it difficult to get out of bed.

But more than all the intricate details he shared with me, I also knew about the only thing that mattered: I was starting to know his heart.

13

A Georgia Kiss On My Mind

On the last day of my whirlwind adventure in Kennesaw, I consciously reminded myself to take in every remaining moment I still had with Declan. Here in the flesh, I was content, and like a little girl, I didn't want to break free from this man who, without rhyme or reason, made me feel so much joy, not even a box full of chocolates and makeup waiting for me back home on my doorstep would have made me happier.

I couldn't believe how fast the weekend had gone by and I almost desperately wanted to call off my never-ending editorial duties at work for a couple more days just to continue waking up to kisses on my forehead and Declan laughing at me every time I butchered the lyrics to Justin Timberlake's recent hit on the radio, *Not A Bad Thing*.

I was leaving heartbroken and sad, yet already attached, even if I didn't dare say so. Declan treated me kinder than Dalai Lama and the Pope combined, and he had been a gentleman this whole time.

Before I left, however, he insisted he had one more thing to show me in town – a surprise I might like – but he wouldn't say what.

"I can help you pack later, but for now, I have a pretty cool place to take you for breakfast. Better than Cracker Barrel. Imagine that!" he exclaimed, dabbing a dime-sized amount of gel over his morning hair as he rushed downstairs to start his car.

I followed his lead, and slipped on my light-blue cardigan sitting by Declan's bed and met him at his noisy, electric-operated garage door. I had no idea where we were going but I fully trusted him and his silly shenanigans at this point.

In a city not too far from Kennesaw called Vinings, known as the prime hub for young professionals out of college, we pulled up to this cute little breakfast joint called the Another Broken Egg café. It was still early in the morning, and since my flight back home was only late that afternoon, we could take our time with breakfast and maybe a quick hike at one town over afterward if we were feeling extra adventurous.

Our server – a young man who looked fresh out of high school and eager to get out into the real world with his way-too-colorful name tag – offered us a booth toward the back of the restaurant, in case we wanted additional privacy away from all the bubbling sounds of poached eggs and hash browns cooking in the kitchen. Declan sat facing me, not even bothering to take a peek at the laminated menu as it became clear to me he was a bit of a regular here. With so many Southern dishes to choose from, I pointed at the one that was everything but.

"I'll have these beignets, please," I said to the server, who had now been patiently waiting for me to place my order for well over a minute. *Yes, beignets for breakfast, because you only live once.* It had been four years since I indulged in these sugary doughnuts. Not since college in New Orleans.

Declan looked like he had something on his mind. Squeezing a slice of lime in his icy-cold glass of water, he briefly glanced over his shoulder as if to get his thoughts together then adjusted his eyes on mine.

"So there's something I've wanted to say to you before you go home today," he began. "I want you to know that in case I forget to tell you this later, I had a really good time with you. I could have never imagined that it would have been this good, just being around you."

"Me neither," I said, smiling back.

I, too, had kept something inside that I needed to say. Something I couldn't shake off and hoped we would share. Although Declan constantly made it a point to show his affection for me during my stay, whether by giving me a surprise peck on the forehead or playfully smacking my butt, there was one thing he hadn't done: He hadn't kiss me on the lips. And come hell or high water, I refused to leave this trip without a kiss from the man who was already starting to mean so much to me. I wanted it more than anything, and at the risk of rejection, I decided to put my big-girl pants on and quit acting shy.

"I want you to know that I want you to kiss me before I go," I suddenly blurted out, almost immediately regretting my out-loud stream of words. "I, uh, I refuse to leave without a kiss."

"Oh, really?" he laughed, unable to hide the blushing grin on his face. "I'm actually so glad you said that. I've been wanting to kiss you since yesterday and wasn't sure if you wanted me to or not. But I'm glad you decided to be that overt with me."

"Well, now you know," I sheepishly responded.

It was towards the end of the afternoon, and my bags were almost fully packed with my less-than-perfectly folded clothes and three-inch heels I ended up not needing after all. In just less than an hour, we would be on our way to the airport, and left to digest everything about the whirlwind magic and craziness of this weekend.

Seeing me trying to squeeze in my pair of dirty, muddy sneakers into an already heavy carry-on that seemed to weigh double than what I had traveled with, Declan came over to the side of his bed where I stood, ready to extend a helping hand.

"Do you need any help?" he asked.

"I'm okay, I got it, thanks." I quietly replied. I was determined to zip up this annoying carry-on suitcase that didn't want to cooperate with me on my own.

"In that case, come here…" he whispered, softly grabbing me by the back of my neck and pulling me close to kiss me. His lips were soft and sweet, just as he had been with me this whole time. And if there was such a thing as butterflies, they hovered around me now and repeatedly took my breath away, as nothing about being with Declan made me feel nervous or afraid.

I wanted to keep him close and to never break away from his stare. I was undeniably intoxicated by his energy, his charm and the impression that for the first time in a long time, I didn't have to run. I could simply be still and let our affection for each other take charge. Something inside of me started to feel real.

Maybe it was the fact that I could now go home with that long-awaited kiss on my mind. Or maybe it was the thought that here, between these two beating hearts, I found a new beginning with a man I never thought I'd meet, yet whom I was starting to realize, was everything I needed in my life.

By the time I arrived back at the Fort Lauderdale airport, it was getting pretty late and inching close to ten. But still unable to come down from my adrenaline high, I called Oceana to see if she had an hour to spare to catch up on some girl talk.

"Of course I do! We have to talk!" she demanded, in the sort of playful way only best friends do. "I wanna hear everything about this trip! Down to the last second you were with him. I'm on my way to the airport. Meet me outside, okay? See you in a bit."

Not many pubs were opened late on a weekday night but Oceana knew just the place for us to go. "I know the owner here so we can just order a couple of beers and hang out," she said as we supported ourselves on a couple of bar stools at a mom-and-pop bar close to her house, the only place that happened to still be open when everybody else was sleeping on a Tuesday.

Oceana's wavy long-length hair flowed naturally against a blowing fan that whirled in her direction, and as I took a sip of my Blue Moon beer, I couldn't help but smile and giggle, even as I tried to cover my mouth and wipe off the stupid grin on my face. I just couldn't stop thinking about him.

"Soooooooo. Tell meeee. I want to know everything!" declared Oceana enthusiastically. "Look at you! Have you even looked at yourself?! You are seriously glowing, Maíra!"

"Gosh, where do I even begin, girl," I wondered. "How do you even begin to describe a dream? Because that's exactly what it felt like. Everything was a dream. Nothing short of a dream. And it was probably one of the best weekends I've ever had. Ever just had a magical moment with someone? I know, it sounds like I've gotten off my rocking chair. But I couldn't have expected it to be as good as it was in person."

I began to delve into every little detail, from how we got stuck in the pouring rain on our hike up Kennesaw Mountain, to how I mustered up the courage to ask Declan to kiss me at the last minute, to how at ease I felt just talking to him late into the night, and finally, to how I managed to slip a note in his hand right before I left, thanking him for everything.

"And there's something else…" I said.

"What?!" she asked, nudging me in the arm. "What is it?? Oooh! I can feel it's something juicy! Tell me!"

"You're going to think I'm crazy but – I really do believe I've met the love of my life. I can't describe it. I can't explain it. But I feel like Declan is my soulmate."

"Wow, girl! Aww. That is so sweet. You wanna know what's crazier? I believe you. I really do. I swear I've never seen you like this, and you know that you and I have been friends for a long time. I'm telling you, I don't know what happened to you, but there is no denying this glow!"

12: 16 a.m. Journal Entry –

On April 27, at around 9 a.m., I met an amazing guy in Kennesaw, Georgia. He is something else. I've been waiting to meet someone like him, and now that I have, I don't want to let him go. Lord, will you keep him close to me? I pray you let this take hold.

14

Memorial Day Weekend

Meeting Declan was the only time I had ever been in the presence of another man who made me feel like I could truly and unapologetically be myself. It was as if I was somehow meant to fly 600 miles just to find him and wipe away anything that came before, and dive in deep to a world of endless possibilities that could take place with him now in sight. Sure, I had loved others in my life but it was never this indescribable, awe-inspiring bond whereby our spirits naturally gravitated toward each other. It was only meeting Declan that I suddenly found myself questioning everything I ever knew.

After my visit to Georgia, we soon thereafter agreed that he'd come see me in Miami next. But scheduling to see each other was no easy task, as we had to be considerate of his time with his daughter, whom stayed with him every other weekend.

"If my ex has Bella Memorial Day Weekend, I promise I'll fly down to Miami to see you, okay?" he assured me.

Barely a year out of his divorce, I was respectful of the fact that most things had to be done on his watch, according to his availability. And that was perfectly okay with me. When Declan did fly out to see me a month after my impromptu visit to Kennesaw, I was more than anxious and bursting with excitement to see him.

Unlike the insane maze of the Atlanta airport, the Fort Lauderdale airport was much smaller, and therefore the gates and terminals were easy to find, even if it was your first time traveling to South Florida. I made plans to pick up Declan by Gate B the Friday before Labor Day weekend, right after the end of my work shift. With only a quarter of gas left in my car, I decided to still confront traffic head on in order to meet Declan at his scheduled arrival time without delay.

Surprisingly, the four-story parking garage at the Fort Lauderdale airport was less crowded than I expected when I pulled up my car next to a line of luggage carts by the elevator and nearby moving walkway. *Maybe most people were smart enough to travel for the long weekend the night before.*

I had arrived fifteen minutes early, but suddenly my cell phone began to flash with a text message as I comfortably rolled down my window and stretched out my aching shoulder blades from the long drive.

"I'm so stoked to see you! I'm about to jump out of my fucking skin! These fuckers better let me off the plane!"

I laughed – I was just as excited to see Declan as he was me.

With sangria flowing and endless servings of sourdough bread dipped in olive oil on our candle-lit table, Declan and I spent the early hours of the evening chowing down at my favorite restaurant called *Tutto Pasta,* an upscale Italian joint in Miami off the corner of Brickell and Coral Way.

I couldn't help but show my excitement in seeing him. My eyes were twinkling brighter than the brightest star in the sky, and Declan's bedtime eyes on mine made me want to jump and down at the sheer joy that we were seeing each other again.

"I know it's only been a month since we saw each other last, but I really missed you," I admitted as I took a swig of another glass of fruit-covered sangria.

"I missed you, too, honey. I still can't believe I'm here."

"I know! About damn time, too, mista."

Finishing off dinner with a tall order of chocolate fudge cake and ice cream, we then made it back to my small efficiency down the street, just five minutes away. I had moved to The Roads neighborhood after getting my most recent job at the digital publishing company I worked for in Wynwood, while also needing a break from everyday traffic.

Situated in a private residential neighborhood, my efficiency was between two others that my landlady had built next to her gated community. On my way to work every day, I usually walked past one of my neighbors, but unlike the rest of the population in Miami, they were quiet and cordial. Living here in The Roads seemed like the perfect place for a single, somewhat goal-oriented woman like me.

"So here it is," I said, pointing out my 250-square-foot efficiency that only managed to fit in my queen bed and an antique dresser of my mother's that stood next to my single apartment mirror.

"Welcome to my humble abode."

Not one to really be surprised or bothered by anything, if Declan felt uncomfortable in my tiny space, he had a good way of hiding it. "Very cute," he said, turning around to see my little dog already pouncing on him to say hello. "It's perfect for just you and Lumee."

"I think so, too. It'll do for now."

"You know what else will do?" he asked, removing his heavy backpack from his shoulders and making himself comfortable on my lavender-scented bedsheets.

"What's that?"

"If you sat right here next to me and kissed me and let me just get my hands on you."

I somehow liked the sound of that, and before I knew it, Declan was pulling me on top of him and pressing his hands on the curves around my hips, as he thrusted his strong body against mine. Without a moment to waste, I was kissing him again and ready to surrender. I had so missed the taste of his lips.

The lights were dim. The door was locked, and the sound of the air conditioning softly hummed in the background as my automated front porch light flickered outside. And while my neighbors were sleeping, we were awake, because the rest of the night was ours to make up for lost time. Up to six times worth of sweat-drenched bedsheets and not a single breath wasted of lost times.

Here, together, Declan suddenly felt every bit mine as our bodies naturally gravitated towards and exploded onto each other and I could no longer tell the passing of time.

With Lumee eager to slobber and lick our faces as soon as the sun came up, we arose early so as not to make the long drive to Broward too late in the day. Dad was throwing a Memorial Day BBQ pool party, and I was anxious to introduce him to my new *friend*.

Dad knew about Declan. And even though I was daddy's little girl as close to daddy's little girl as you can get – starting from the time I crawled out of diapers and uttered *dadda* as my first word much to the disappointment of my mother – dad wasn't the type to stop me from going out and experiencing life myself. Since he also often stayed up-to-date with my dating shenanigans, it seemed only natural that I finally tell him about the "special Georgia guy" I recently met.

By the time we arrived to my dad's house an hour after I told him I would, several family friends were already singing and hollering who-knows-what out by the swimming pool. Dad had purchased this home in the city of Sunrise just four years prior, and after remodeling it down to the hand-built, long-stretching wooden cabinets he wanted behind his washer and dryer in the garage, it was a place he took great pride in.

"Hey, guys! Come on in!" said dad, as we made our way toward the smell of freshly-grilled hamburgers and baked potatoes cooking outside by the ironed linen-covered patio table. Both family and friends alike had gathered for the long holiday weekend occasion, feasting at whatever delicious sausages and patties they could get their hands on and red plastic cups filled with your alcohol of choice. But as soon as people began to take notice of the strange man who was holding my hand as we entered, the room suddenly grew quiet and everybody stood still.

One by one, family friends began to gawk at Declan, a person they could have assumed I pulled out of a modeling catalog. I knew what they were all thinking. I was used to it by now. And as they poked and probed him about his life, Declan somehow remained nonchalant and chill and answered their questions with ease.

Yes, I grew up in Florida before moving to Georgia.

Yes, my family is from Spain.

Yes, I have a daughter.

Yes, I'm a military baby.

Even dad was impressed. "My daughter has said many nice things about you. She really wanted me to meet you, so I thank you for coming," he said, patting Declan on the back.

"The pleasure is all mine, sir. Thank you so much for having me in your home."

Once the *"ooohs!"* and *"that's so cool!"* started to die down, Declan and I took a second to sneak away and pull out a couple of chairs by the swimming pool and enjoy some moments to ourselves. While the kids played with squirt guns and animal-shaped floats, and the adults cracked jokes and grumbled about the intense South Florida summer humidity, Declan seemed unfazed, quietly holding my hand and taking in the vibrant, lively atmosphere around him. Blissful and carefree, we were devouring a slice of tropical paradise that neither one of us could complain.

Then, just as I was about to rest my head on Declan's chest and take in the surroundings myself, I felt somebody knock me out of my heavenly daze and brush up against me.

"Hey Maíra! Mind if I steal you inside for a second?"

Nance, an old family friend in her fifties whom I had known for several years, was one to always speak her mind whenever she was around. I didn't see her often as I would have liked to. With her event planning business in Broward, and my living in Miami, making time for each other started to become reserved only for special occasions such as this.

"Sure," I said. "Declan, I'll be right back, I promise." I hoped I hadn't made this any more awkward that it probably already was.

Pulling me in to my dad's disorganized office and closing the creaking door behind her, Nance told me to have a seat. *Uh-oh, this can't be good.* Sensing the worried look on my face, she giggled. "Oh, not to worry. It's nothing bad I wanted to talk to you about."

"Okay…. So, what is it? Is there something going on?"

"Oh, no no. I was just trying to find an excuse to pull you aside to say how happy you look! I know we haven't seen each other in a while but I've been observing you since the moment you got here with this man, and well – I may not know much about the two of you, but it is clear to me you are smitten!"

"Aww, Nance. So that's what you called me in here for. You had me worried for a second."

"Told you it was nothing bad," she reassured me. "You guys just make a beautiful couple and I had to tell you that."

"That's so sweet of you, Nance. Really. But you should probably know that we're unfortunately not together…" I said, trying to clear up her innocent assumption. "We're just casually seeing each other."

"Sure you are. I understand. That's how it always starts. Just allow yourself to go with the flow and the rest will come naturally," she reminded me, flashing a smile that showed off her pearly whites. "I learned a long time ago in my youth to never ask a guy any questions. And if nothing works out between you two, at least now you know you will have learned something from all of this."

"And what's that?"

"You see a guy like him? That's the kind of person you need in your life. A mature, older guy like him."

I could only nod in agreement. Even though months had gone by since I had seen Nance, I knew she was right. I was starting to fall for Declan, and it seemed like everybody else around me knew it too.

The next evening, Declan and I stopped at a hole-in-the-wall bar just a couple of blocks from the Italian restaurant I introduced him to. We were exhausted from our weekend adventures, and after staying late in Broward to help my father clean up the BBQ mess, we decided we would just take it easy on Declan's last night in town. Just a good draft beer anywhere nearby would do.

"This is probably my favorite bar ever," I told Declan as we walked inside Blackbird Ordinary, a hidden gem I liked to sometimes venture off to on Sunday evenings when other kids were still recovering from their hangovers of the previous night.

Only about half a dozen people wearing bare-to-nothing clothes in the summer heat were ordering drinks inside, quietly talking amongst themselves while asking the bartender about the latest draft on tap. Still feeling rather tired, Declan and I hadn't even cared enough to get properly dressed like everybody else who swooned and whispered around us. Dressed in our casual wear, we found an available booth in the back of the bar and began ordering a couple of beers on tap ourselves.

I was about to excuse myself to the ladies' restroom, before Declan and I ordered another round, when, from the corner of my eye, I could see him taking a hard, good look at a stranger who seemed to be drunkenly gazing in our direction.

"Did you see that guy over there checking you out?" pointed out Declan. Not exactly knowing what he was talking about and seeing no indication that an unknown man was flirting with me, I resumed getting up to go to the bathroom and laughed it off.

"You're probably seeing things, silly. I assure you that guy is not looking my way."

"Ohhhh, yes, he was," he reaffirmed. But before I had a second to say anything more, Declan leaned over, poking his head over our booth and playfully yelling out, "Yeah, I know she's hot, and what!"

Oh no he didn't just say that. Completely caught off guard, I tried to play it cool by hiding my face behind the peeling wrapper of the beer bottle in front of me. Not one to shy away from speaking his mind, there was Declan going at it and making wisecracks again. Yet, as momentarily embarrassed as I was, his random outburst was also one of the most endearing things about him. Because even when Declan's filter-less brain got the best of him, all I could do was laugh.

Soon our time together in South Florida started coming to an end, and I hated being put in the position where I had to part ways with Declan once again. *How did these days go by so fast? Why did we have to say goodbye?* I knew I was already becoming attached and he could see it, too.

It was the morning of his flight back home, and Declan could see the sadness in my eyes as he looked up at me while packing his last batch of clothes in his backpack. We had just spent all of Memorial Day weekend together, and yet it felt like no time at all. Our time together wasn't enough, and I hated that I had to bear the torture of saying goodbye once more.

Sensing the change in my demeanor, Declan put away one final loose-hanging shirt he hadn't even worn during his trip, then grabbed my hand, nudging me to look at him.

"You seem sad, I can tell. You doing okay?"

"It just gets harder and harder every time I have to say goodbye to you. And I don't know if you feel it too."

"I do. I hate it too. There's no denying I love being around you," he said. "When I'm with you, I feel like I'm the happiest I've been in a very long time. Who knows, maybe after a couple more visits, I'll be your permanent boy and we can make this thing between us more permanent."

"I know we're nothing serious, but – Declan, I don't wanna lose you." I was almost in tears, surprised by the emotional attachment I had already developed with him.

"I know, sweetie," he said. His fingers were now trickling up and down my arm and caressing the back of my neck. "Listen, I have three important things going on in my life right now: my daughter, my health and school. But I don't want it to end there. In due time, I'd like you to eventually play a role in my life too. And I want you to know something else: You're the only person I'm seeing and that's not going to change."

Managing to finally release a smile, I knew that was all I needed to hear. As long as Declan felt the same as I did, that was enough for me. But I also understood that we both had to be patient with time and let things unravel naturally as they should.

I understood that the foundation of this relationship would require more from us due to the distance. I understood that sacrifices would need to be made. But I was willing to give it all the minutes of every hour, as long as I found myself with him in the end. And I hoped he felt the same.

The week after Declan returned home, however, things took an unexpected turn. Almost out of nowhere, it seemed as if now it was his demeanor – and not mine – that seemingly appeared to change. Without explanation, our everyday talks became significantly shorter and the enthusiasm in his voice faded to non-existence. Since we were both getting back to our day-to-day lives, I shrugged it off to him simply returning to his regular, mundane routine. After all, work had the tendency to snap us back to reality. Or so I thought.

But like a woman's intuition poking you right in the face until you finally give way and listen, I could no longer dismiss or deny Declan's sharp distance with me. From going through 48-hour periods without a single text to not knowing when I would speak to him next, I could suddenly tell something was definitely up – something he wasn't telling me.

Eventually, after much persistence, Declan confided in me that he was wrestling with getting back in the dating field again. It still felt too soon, he said. Although he and Bella's mom had been separated for months, their recent divorce was something he admittedly was still coming to terms with.

"I need to focus on the three things I can control in my life," he texted me a week after coming to Miami to see me. "I apologize for this, Maíra. I know it sucks, and it irritates me and pains me that I'm not ready yet. But I'm just not."

I couldn't believe it. How could he call us off just like that when our relationship was still in the bare beginnings of a honeymoon phase? Didn't he just say he loved being around me and wanted me in his life? How could he shut off his feelings like that? I didn't understand and I wasn't sure I even wanted to understand. But instead of letting my emotions fly high and going after him like one of those persons, I spent the afternoon following his hard-to-hear news rocking myself underneath a palm tree by my landlady's swimming pool.

Earlier in the day, I purchased a bottle of blush wine that I now knew the perfect occasion to use it for. I poured it into a water bottle I disguised as fruit punch and took a hard swig. No, make that several hard swigs. One by one, I downed them all as much as I could, letting the taste of the fruit punch settle in my throat and the alcohol effects take me by surprise. And I sat there, looking out into the unknown, startled at how drastically everything changed. *Just like that.*

I wondered how it was possible that a week ago Declan rested his body on mine, and now I had to retreat myself to this cold and cruel unforgiveable silence. Without a second thought, I drowned my sorrows into the pool and opened up my heartache to the sky. As I took a puff of my e-cigarette, I begrudgingly wished I could smoke Declan up and away. Somewhere far, far away into the deepest corners of the Universe. I was tormented by the memory of his kisses. But, most of all, I was tormented for feeling like a *damn* fool.

I could not shake off the feeling that I lost the one man who truly *got me*. In turn, I did the only thing I knew how to do: I cried my eyes out for weeks, and then. It all stopped. Suddenly, there were no more clove cigarettes or bottles of wine that could continue to numb my pain. And *fuck,* it felt nearly impossible to see past my pain. It felt impossible to even consider that someday I would look back at this heartache and swing my finger at God and internally cry out, *you, jokester, you.* But as it were, *somebody* was still on my side. *Somebody* who had bigger plans than I could foresee.

But for that, I had to wait.

Two years would go by before Declan and I saw each other again.

PART IV –

The Reveal

"Time and you, it made me love,
it made me love more."

Theme song from the movie Comet

15

Full Circle

*D*ay 30: Love agrees in prayer. Use this time to commit your concerns and needs to Him.

With a fresh load of laundry done, I dropped off Lumee at my father's apartment early in the evening. My flight to see Declan again for his birthday, and ultimately reveal the Love-Dare challenge, was set for the next day. I had just put my last pair of clean jeans up to hang inside my bedroom closet. Some dresses were packed in my suitcase, and the *Fireproof* DVD my friend Greg let me borrow stared at me from the front pocket of my luggage. He had given it to me again just for the sake of this trip.

The Love-Dare challenge scrapbook I painstakingly put together for the past month had all but the last page filled. I had reserved it for something special: a picture of Declan and me from his visit to Miami two years ago, taken at that Memorial Day BBQ pool party. "I was so happy that day," he remarked during one of our recent memory-lane conversations. "I was happy and carefree with you."

I knew that while I fondly now regarded this year of reconnecting with Declan as one of my best, I imagined Declan would say otherwise due to so many unexpected and uninvited events in his life. The greater part of the year was one I imagined he wished to toss into a bottle, out in to the open sea and never to be seen again. But there was also a light in all the darkness.

Declan could breathe a sigh of relief after receiving notification from his attorney saying that his second divorce was settled, just a few days after our trip to Melbourne. *He never had to be under the same roof with her again.* He was relieved that he managed to be there for his family during the untimely passing of his brother. *He never had to live with feelings of guilt.* And he was relieved that he could still go to work with his head held high and still tackle all the responsibilities of his day-to-day life, even if he was still in pain.

But the truth is, just as much as Declan had one foot forward, the other foot was still left dangling behind him. A long road to healing and recovery lied ahead before he could even think about taking off his shoes and walking barefoot on solid land.

Growing up, I looked forward to my birthdays for one reason, and one reason alone: My mother made a grand spectacle of them every year, starting from the time I turned 5 and the ballroom of our apartment building was transformed into a *My Little Pony* dazzling wonderland. But it didn't end there. From the moment the dial on the clock hit midnight and my cell phone rang not a second later, to the cards and birthday gifts mom placed on my bed in the morning, birthdays were made to be a big deal. Because why not. She treated every year of life as a celebration, as it should be.

I carried my mother's enthusiasm for birthdays with me as I got older. When she passed, I stopped celebrating my own, but the celebration of others remained a big deal to me. I didn't want Declan to spend his birthday alone. He had been through so much. I wanted him for one day to embrace what he meant to others, and what he meant to me.

We made plans for me to fly back up to Georgia on a Thursday night, just a few days shy of his 42nd birthday. I would work remotely that Friday then surprise him with a million and one little surprises. Yet, as excited as I felt, I was also almost sick to my stomach.

For the past three months, I mastered the art of hiding my own feelings. I took on the role of a friend but I could no longer keep this growing love for him to myself. I promised myself at the beginning of the Love-Dare challenge that after those 30 days, I would let go. I was wearing my heart on my sleeve while inching toward the verge of falling apart.

My late-night flight to Atlanta from the Fort Lauderdale airport, the closest airport to me, was surprisingly half empty. After requesting to switch seats to a spot towards the front of the plane, I now had an entire row to myself. I always hated waiting a good 30 minutes before I could finally walk down the terminal upon landing. No, this time, I made it a point to get out as soon as possible. *It was Declan's upcoming birthday* I wanted to tell the flight attendant, but instead I attempted to telepathically convey this message to her and hope that she understood.

"Good evening, ladies and gentlemen. Our flight to Atlanta Hartsfield-Jackson International Airport will be approximately an hour and 27 minutes. We have clear skies tonight. So sit back and relax. We hope you enjoy your flight. On behalf of Delta, thank you for flying with us tonight."

I wondered how many people on the plane were experiencing any kind of inner turmoil in their lives, much like my own. Or did only happy people board planes? Were flights only often made up of individuals who were in a good place in their lives and were flying to celebrate a momentous event, to take advantage of a long vacation or perhaps to be reunited with a loved one? Was I the only one who could not compartmentalize my emotions and just be at ease?

The left wing of the plane steadied itself as we flew deep into a cotton field of clouds. Not a star was in sight. Not even the blinking lights on the wing itself. Although I had already been to Georgia multiple times before, this time I started to get nervous. I pictured every scenario I could in my head about what Declan's reaction would be once I came clean about the Love Dare. Instead of acting like a confident woman in my thirties, I was suddenly 15 again. A silly 15-year-old girl whose life depended upon whether the boy she liked, liked her back.

Soon the flight attendants began their rounds of offering beverages and a small bag of pretzels, not bigger than the size of my hand, to passengers onboard.

"Ma'am, would you like anything to drink?" asked the older one of the two female flight attendants. With perfect white teeth, she had such a pristine smile you wondered if she was a dentist in a previous life.

"Yes, please. I'll have a Merlot. Actually, make that two. Charge it on this card," I said, handing over my MasterCard.

If she thought I was crazy for requesting two glasses of wine, one after the other, on an 11 p.m. flight, she did her best not to show. I opened my flimsy seat tray and placed the two cups of wine in front of me. There wasn't enough room for me to place my leather-bound journal that I carried with me at all times at this point. I guess I would have to drink first before I could write. It was as if I had to choose between the lesser of two evils.

With my bulky Bluetooth headphones over my head, I turned on one of my Spotify playlists and looked out the window. I needed to listen to some music to relax. I needed to pray and surrender to any higher force that would listen to me in this night sky.

"I'm distracted by the noise, just trying to make sense of all your promises. Sometimes I gotta stop and remember that you're God and I am not. I know you see me. I know you hear me, Lord. Your plans are for me. Goodness you have in store. So, thy will be done... thy will be done."

I sighed as Lady Antebellum's Hillary Scott's voice began to echo in my head. I had recently stumbled upon her newest single of her new Christian family album. It was a song she wrote after suffering a miscarriage. But even through her personal pain, it was her hope that others could find solace in her words and comfort in her voice.

"Hello, ladies and gentlemen. It is your captain speaking again. We have begun our descent into the Atlanta airport and will be arriving in about 20 minutes. Please put your seat in the upright position and clear of any belongings from

the aisle. Whether or not Atlanta is your final destination, we hope you enjoyed your flight and hope to see you with Delta again soon."

One final sip of wine and I was ready to land.

The entryway to Declan's mansion-of-a-house remained untouched when I arrived. An Amazon shipping box still sat on top of an antique bench in the corridor. Bella's cheerleading bag with her name engraved on the front was next to it. Just as he did every time before, Declan carried my luggage upstairs, as I checked to see what clothes I left behind in a guest closet from my previous visits. He still had my bag of gym wear untouched and unmoved, just waiting for my return.

"I have to tell you I've got a few surprises up my sleeve this weekend," I exclaimed. "I hope you're ready!"

We were hanging out in his living room after I dropped off my stuff in Bella's room, then made myself comfortable on Declan's chest as we rested on a foam-cushioned couch I had now taken a personal liking to. I always loved pressing my head on Declan's stomach and feeling his five-times-a-week workout build and heart beat against my ear. He no longer had this tense, distressed look upon his face. It was nice to see him looking more peaceful and at ease, as if he felt comforted by the fact that he could now resume his normal life.

"I guess I have no choice but to be ready, huh? It's funny, I never know what to expect with you," he said with a twinge of nervousness yet excitement, while he ran his fingers through the wavy curls of my hair. "So I was thinking. After I'm done with work tomorrow, how about we go to the local bar and grab a bite to eat? I know you want me to watch that *Fireproof* movie you've been talking about so we can do that after. Maybe open a bottle of wine and just hang out here. What do you think?"

"Sure, that sounds good! I'm for up anything, you know me. And remember, we have to make the most of this weekend. It's your birthday! And birthdays only come once a year," I reminded him.

"Hmm. I wonder what you're up to. So just so you know, I'll leave the extra key by the front door in case you need to go somewhere during the day. I'll feed Ozzy before I head to work, so you don't have to worry about that. I know you just got here and I don't mean to be a dick, but it's late and I'm tired, hun. Ready for bed?"

"No worries. I'm tired too. That flight was super long and I'm sorry I ended up getting here so late. Goodnight, sweetie. I'll be here when you get off work tomorrow," I said, getting up to go brush my teeth in the hallway bathroom.

"Hey, not so fast!" he said. "Come here, give me a hug goodnight."

As he pulled me in to wrap his arms around my straighened back, I didn't want him to let go. Because every time Declan put his arms around me, I felt like I was in a place where I belonged. While some say it's a person's eyes or smile that draws them in, it was his hugs that I always looked forward to.

Cracks of sunlight peeked through the corners of the curtain panel in Bella's room on the second floor. I checked the time on my cell phone. It was 8 a.m. and Declan had already left for work at his Manager of Sales Operation job in greater Atlanta. As for me, it was time to get down to business. Serious birthday business.

Ozzy was quick to follow me downstairs as I grabbed plastic store bags of birthday decorations I secretly stashed inside my luggage. Just a day earlier, hours before my flight, I ran to the local Publix and picked up whatever cute birthday signs and stickers I could find.

I took a look around me. Declan's kitchen and living room were interconnected with no hallway in between them. Since I wasn't your typical house fashionista by any means, and I had no good eye for any kind of interior design, I wondered what would be the best way for me to go about putting up these decorations.

A large *Happy Birthday* banner could fit across one side of Declan's living room to the other, just around the top corners of a long wall that stretched over his rarely used fireplace. Another banner could easily go over the fireplace itself. Cheesy birthday hats were to be placed on the kitchen table and sugar cookies would be made at some point throughout the day. But there was one more thing: a letter. I had to also write Declan a letter.

"From the moment you walk into this house, we will begin your birthday celebration. For the next few days, let's have a little bit of fun. It's been a rough couple of months, but for today, no stress is allowed. This is your time to enjoy yourself! So kick off your shoes! It's time to celebrate your life. Happy Birthday to the most awesome guy I know!"

So, I admit, I was perhaps a bit overenthusiastic putting up these birthday decorations without knowing what the heck I was doing – but I wanted to make his birthday special. Even at the sake of pinning silly streamers over his fireplace. Declan and I had never spent his birthday together, and though this was the first time, I wasn't sure if it would be the last. *Every moment counts.*

Late that afternoon, I heard Declan's car pull up into the garage with its loud engine roaring behind it. Ozzy was already by the door, his tail excitedly wagging back and forth, waiting for his dad to come inside and pat him on the head. "Hey buddy," he greeted him, dropping his house keys on the floor to pet his four-legged friend.

I was in the kitchen trying to bake some birthday sugar cookies, only to find myself failing miserably in the process. Wiping my hands clean with a paper towel, I then came out into the hallway to find Declan reading my letter then quizzically looking around him.

"This is all so nice of you," he said, pointing to the decorations that somehow still stood in place. "Nobody has ever done anything like this for me before. I was actually having a bad day until I came in and saw all this and read your letter. Thank you."

I smiled and told him there were some half-baked sugar cookies on the counter, in case he wanted to give them a go. As fit as he was, I still knew Declan wasn't ever the type to say *no* to cookies.

Old Towne and Tavern Bar and Grill, sandwiched between a run-down tattoo parlor and a thrift store in the heart of Kennesaw, was probably Declan's favorite spot in town, especially after a long day. I had been here before a couple of times so it kind of also became my favorite place to crack open a beer and unwind. Similar to a typical sports bar you would find in South Florida, there were large flat-screen TVs overhead and signs of super cheap drink specials taunting you to get more.

Declan and I opted to sit right at the bar with a soccer game playing on one of the screens, instead of at one of the tight spaces in a surrounding booth. While I ordered my standard Blue Moon beer, Declan went straight for the whiskey.

"I hate whiskey," I remembered once telling him. "I don't know why many people like it. Bleh. It's so strong." Who would think of being around a girl who didn't like whiskey, right? I could see an imaginary buzzer going off with a big, fat "X" on my forehead. *Bzzzzz... you're out.*

"So, I have to tell ya," he began after putting his glass of whiskey down as if needing a moment to think about what he wanted to say. "I'm often sharing my darkest secrets with you, but I would like for you to be vulnerable with me, too." How typical. One whiskey in and we were already straight shooting toward the heavy stuff of not-so-casual conversations.

The opportunity to open up and allow myself to be fully raw and unfiltered lay before me. If I wanted Declan to trust me and consider me one of his closest friends, I had to be willing to share, too. And so, I began revealing stories of my past – past mistakes and struggles I still carried with me. Haunting stories I couldn't let go of. Difficult memories that would wake me up at night and crawl into bed with me. Stories that could be regarded as both embarrassing and shameful that maybe only two other people in my life knew about. Then, as I rounded off every little detail I could, I didn't know whether I should let out a sigh of relief or dash toward the first emergency exit sign before facing the potential possibility that he may never want to talk to me again.

"That's it?!" he remarked when I was done. "Hey, that's not bad at all hun. Like, at all. Shit happens."

I shrugged, surprised by his reaction.

Our conversation then turned to talk about me possibly moving to Georgia. I could see Declan didn't really know how to actually come out and say that was something that had been on his mind.

"Do you remember a couple of years ago, when we first met, how I suggested you move up here?" he said, before asking for another glass of whiskey.

"Yeah."

"I'll have you know that my thoughts on that haven't changed. I would love to have you here. I think you would do well in Georgia. You would fit right in. Besides, I would then have my best friend close to me."

"Best friend, as in me?"

"Of course you, silly girl."

"Aww. That's so sweet. Well, I'll have you know that I've considered moving here to be honest with you," I reassured him. "I've been wanting to leave Florida for a long time. I'm tired of the people there and the cost of living is draining me. Plus there's a million other reasons why I want to leave. I just don't think now is the right time. I'd have to get a job here first."

"You know I'd take you in, in a heartbeat. You can always stay with me – rent free – until you get settled," he said, looking at me as if he meant serious business.

"You're sweet. You always know how to make me feel at home. If I get a job opportunity in Georgia, I won't think twice to move."

"Promise?"

"Promise."

I couldn't let Declan know the truth that my eyes and mind were already set on moving to Georgia, not because of a potential career move, but because I wanted to be with him. But I chalked it up to needing a job first, even if that really wasn't even an issue for me. A couple of Blue Moon beers later, though, I was clearly already lying through my teeth.

It was almost completely dark out by the time we made it back to his house. Ozzy had found his comfy resting place on the armrest of the sofa, as Declan rummaged through the kitchen to pour himself a drink. Maybe Scotch on the rocks, followed by some wine now that we were home.

"Are we still watching *Fireproof?*" I asked, making my way close to Ozzy.

"Yeah, of course, we can watch it now if you want."

I sat on the carpeted floor in the living room as Declan turned on the DVD player and hit "play" on the remote control. For some reason, I hesitated to watch the movie on the couch next to him. Who was I kidding, I was already a bundle of nerves and I just couldn't bring myself to be in such close proximity with the man who would soon know about these deep-rooted feelings I had been hiding for months. With the coffee table between us, I secured my legs up to my chest and braced myself for how the next two hours might unfold.

Fireproof doesn't mean the fire will never come. It means when the fire comes that you will be able to withstand it.

Scene 18 –

Catherine is sick in bed and has been for days. Michael knocks on the bedroom door, then enters and sits by her bedside. He gives her a beverage from her favorite fast food joint, Chik-Fil-A. She takes a sip then looks up at him.

Catherine: Why are you doing this?

Caleb: I've learned that you never leave your partner, especially in a fire.

Catherine: Caleb, what's happened to you?

Caleb sighs then answers: Dad gave me something. I can let you read it.

Catherine pulls out a [Love-Dare] journal from her nightstand: Was it this?

Caleb: How long have you known?

Catherine: I found it yesterday. So what day are you on?

Caleb: 43.

Catherine: But there's only 40.

Caleb: Who says I have to stop?

Catherine: I don't know how to process this. This is not normal for you.

Caleb: Welcome to the new normal.

Catherine: You didn't want to do this at first, did you?

Caleb: No. But halfway through, I realized that I did not understand what love was. And once I understood what it is, I wanted to do it.

Caleb gets down on his knee and takes an apologetic stance: I need you to understand something. I am sorry. I have been so selfish. For the past seven years I have trampled on you with my words and my actions. I have loved other things when I should have loved you.

And the last few weeks God has given me a love for you I never had before. I've asked him to forgive me and I am hoping, I am praying that somehow you would be able to forgive me, too. I do not want to live the rest of my life without you.

Scene 21 –

Catherine appears at the fire station where Caleb works. He is surprised to see her. Before he can say a word, she approaches him from a distance.

Catherine: If I haven't told you that you are a good man, you are. If I haven't told you that I've forgiven you, I have. And if I haven't told you that I love you, I do. Something has changed in you, Caleb, and I want what happened to you to happen to me.

The final scene of *Fireproof* was playing on the screen, and while Declan continued watching as the end credits began to roll, I, on the other hand, found myself inconsolable and crying uncontrollably. The sleeves of my cute, buttoned-up shirt were run down with tears and snot, all in one, spilling from my runny nose. I looked a wreck, but I couldn't stop the tears from streaming down my face. And now I was also shaking.

For the past 30 days, the Love-Dare challenge had taken a life of its own inside me. I had purposefully lived and breathed every direction and guidance it provided, no matter how far or how deep it made me go. Both through the *Fireproof* movie and my scrapbook. Now it had all come to this. To this moment where I could no longer hold back or turn to run away. All that was left of me were these feelings I could no longer hide and my insides stripped to the core.

I was, in two words, completely vulnerable. Just as Declan asked me to be a few hours earlier. I felt myself crawling in my own skin, so without even taking one look at Declan, I positioned myself off the floor and turned my back away from the television screen. I didn't want him to see me like this for any longer than what he probably already had.

"Are you okay?" he asked, as the muffled sounds of my tears began to cause concern. "Maíra – look at me – are you okay?"

"There's something I need to give you, Declan," I responded, turning back around and trying to control my sobs.

"Yes, sure, of course. Anything. Do you wanna go outside? Maybe get some fresh air?"

I followed him to the back porch and propped up one of his patio chairs on a patch of grass. The cool night looked clear outside with just a faint sound of crickets who knows where. The stars twinkled high above the clouds, almost as if to let me know they were here, in the background, just waiting to comfort me should I need them to.

Ozzy had joined us too, roaming around Bella's trampoline and sniffing for a spot to pee, while Declan lit a clove cigarette that had been smushed in the back pocket of his pants. He was leaning back now on a chair next to me, waiting until I felt comfortable enough to speak. I could tell he was starting to worry.

The tears wouldn't stop but the gentle softness in his eyes told me it was okay to say whatever it is I needed to say.

Before the movie started, as Declan was pouring himself a glass of Scotch, I had tucked my Love-Dare challenge scrapbook by a window in his kitchen. I grabbed it before we went outside and pulled it from behind me now and placed it on his lap. The front cover still looked presentable, as well as unstained and unaffected by my tears.

To: Declan

From: Maíra

Love-Dare Activity (31 Days)

July 11 – August 10th, 2016

"Declan," I began, still trying to think of how I would get my words out straight. "You know how I've been saying I can't tell you anything when you've wanted so much for me to be vulnerable."

"Yeah," he said, not quite understanding.

"Well, you know I've also said how it would all make sense to you in time, right? There's a reason for that, Declan. There's a reason why I haven't been able to be vulnerable with you – until now."

I paused and took a deep breath before continuing.

"Okay, let me just come out and say it. I – I- I've been doing the Love-Dare challenge with you for the past 31 days," I sobbed.

"What?!" he gasped, almost knocking his cigarette on Ozzy.

"Are you serious?" I had never seen Declan in shock, but here, there was no denying how taken a-back he was by my revelation.

"Yes," I quietly replied. "Just like the movie. It's all chronicled in this scrapbook. Every dare I did. And I know what you're going to say, Declan. I know what excuses you are going to give me, and I'm not in an emotional place to deal with it. So please. Just read through the scrapbook and don't give me a reaction."

"I just wanted you to have this," I cried, still panting in between my breaths. "And then we can move on. I'm gonna get up now so you can read it privately."

I was about to walk back inside his house when Declan stood up and stretched out his hand in front of my chest to stop me. "Maíra, wait," he said. "Before you go, there is something I need to tell you. And it's not a reaction you're expecting."

With my eyes lowered to the ground, too afraid to look up at him and feel my heart shatter into a thousand pieces, I did the only thing I could do. I wiped my tears as I continued to cry. *Prepare for the worst, Maíra. He is going to reject you.*

Declan began flicking his clove cigarette back and forth in an unsteady pace of hesitation. I could almost feel the tension and sweat build in his hands. Seconds went by, then minutes. Silence. More silence. My eyes still firmly on the ground. *Okay, this can't be good.*

"Maíra," he finally said. "So. It just so happened that I told a co-worker of mine this week that I have a friend I – well – that I know I'm going to marry someday. And that friend I was talking about is you."

"What?!" I blurted out, wondering if I had mistaken what I just heard.

"Yes, just what I said. Don't you see? I love you, Maíra," he continued, now standing so close to me I could almost feel his heart beat pulsate with mine, as tears also formed in his eyes. "And there's more. All those times I told you 'I love you,' whether it was via the phone, by text or whenever I saw you – it wasn't on the basis of friendship. No. I've wanted you to see this for the longest time – I've wanted you to see that I'm committed to you. And before I even open this scrapbook, I wanted you to know this. Because, regardless of what is in this scrapbook, it does not change how I feel about you. I'm not running away, not this time. *You're so beautiful to me, baby girl…"*

If I hadn't been crying hard enough before, I was now drowning in a flood of tears.

"Are you serious?! Is this real?! Somebody pinch me!" I half-heartedly laughed before grabbing him and kissing him passionately on the lips. I wanted to kiss him so hard that nobody and nothing would ever come between us again. I wanted to ravage him with so much ardor and love he wouldn't know what to do with himself.

"Declan, I love you! I so *fucking* love you. I am crazy and madly and just –ugh – so insanely in love with you!"

I could now finally shout my feelings to the world! And I didn't care if the neighbors heard my stupid cries or sudden outbursts of joy. Overwhelmed with emotion, I was living my dream come true, and it was better than how I could have ever imagined.

With Declan's cigarette now left in particles on the patio floor, Ozzy began to bark, wondering what all this commotion was about. I still had a hard time composing myself. I couldn't stop kissing the man of my dreams who now looked at me so lovingly, and giggled and smiled seeing such happiness plastered all over my face.

"Oh, honey. This is one of the things I love the most about you. You've got the biggest heart of anybody I know," he said, as I finally let him pull away from one of my kisses.

After taking a couple of moments to blot my face with tissues and remove traces of my fuchsia lipstick from his mouth, I reclined back on my chair, as Declan pulled up his next to me. One page at a time, I watched him flip through the scrapbook, concentrating on every word, every declaration of love that was now his to keep:

Page 2 – Day 3: Love is comforting. Give him a compliment today or say an encouraging word. I told you today of how I find it so beautiful to see the kind of amazing father you are. Your love for Bella is unmatched.

Page 7 – Day 11: Love cherishes. Do something today that meets a need of his. I flew up to Georgia and drove down eight hours to Melbourne with you. Grief is a bitch.

Page 8 – Day 13: Love fights fair. Write out a list of things that have angered you or upset you, then ask God for patience and wisdom to let them go. I'm scared that you will go away again. I'm upset that those who did not deserve you had your heart in the past. I'm scared you may never give us the change we deserve.

Page 12 – Day 16: Love intercedes. Pray for three specific areas in his life where you desire for God to work. I pray that you see everything you need is standing before you. I pray that you are given the right opportunity to help others. I pray that the Lord remove your insecurities and fears.

Page 13 – Day 17: Love is impossible. Look back over the dares from the previous days. Were there some that seemed impossible? Day 12 and 13 were hard. I was trying so hard to be there for you and your family, but inside I was crying every night in the guest room. Because it was in Melbourne that I realized how strongly I was falling for you.

Page 22 – Day 31: Write a letter of commitment.

I could tell Declan was speechless and struggling to find any words. All he could do was embrace me and pull me toward him, as I looked up at him with such longing. The long drives to Melbourne. The countless on-the-fly flights to Georgia. The sleepless nights. The heavy the heart. The agonizing pain. The crazy unknown. The what-ifs. It had all been worth it. It had all brought us to this moment that I wouldn't change for anything in this world.

The shimmering stars now swirled around us and welcomed a sense of peace that rested and resided inside of me. I was floating toward a light that shined brighter than the brightest star in the sky whenever he looked at me. And here, experiencing a love I had never known before, I found pure ecstasy in its embrace.

An hour or so later, Declan and I settled back on the couch inside, away from the cool air that started to get cold. His arms were always around me now, and nothing could possibly feel more right. We had found the perfect opportunity to open up and share without a care in the world. There was nothing that could make either of us turn away.

We continued to reveal ourselves to each other, asking questions that we kept buried deep inside. Whether it was talk about how we wanted to create our future together or talk about more crazy things we had done in the past, or romantic things and sexual things we wanted to explore together, nothing was off the table.

"Babe, so I have to tell you. I was so nervous about revealing myself to you. The truth is, I wasn't sure if you saw me more than just a friend," I said, taking a sip of his third round of Scotch and already feeling comfortable enough to assign him a pet name. "Especially when you would tell me about and describe the 'right person' in your life."

"Oh, honey. No, you misunderstood. When I spoke of the so-called 'right person,' I guess you can say I was testing you in a way," he explained. "I wanted to give you the opportunity to walk away if you thought being with me – with all my baggage – would be too much for you. I didn't want you to ever feel pressured to stay."

He scooted the glass of Scotch between us to the side, turned my face toward his and then kissed me softly once more. "My heart is with you, only you."

As the night started to wind down, and Ozzy retreated upstairs to his bed and the soothing sounds of the ceiling fan in the master bedroom, Declan asked if we could hold hands and pray over the start of this new relationship. Clasping our hands in prayer, I happily obliged.

Lord, bless us as we embark on this new chapter in our lives. Show us how to move forward by trusting You and Your timing. Thank you for bringing Maira and I together again. May the love we have for each other light the way. Today, and for all days. Show us the path to building our future together and growing in our fondness and adoration for each other. We ask this in Jesus' name. Amen.

"Amen," I whispered, proclaiming our love out into the Universe.

I instantly found myself yawning now, as the emotions and excitement of the night slowly started to let us know that it was time for bed.

"Ready to go to bed?"

"Yeah, let's go. It's been such a crazy, awesome night but we're both getting tired, for sure. After you, babe," I said, getting up from the couch and holding Declan's hand as he led me upstairs. I was about to retreat to his daughter's room for the night as I had done every time before when he suddenly stopped me.

"Do you wanna sleep in my room tonight?" he asked, turning his head toward his open bedroom door on the far side of the corridor. "Since, you know, we are a couple now after all…"

I couldn't believe he could be so considerate and sweet, already thinking about how to seamlessly make me feel like *his girl.*

Following Declan into his room, I retrieved an oversized t-shirt from his closet, while he took off his shirt, exposing his bare chest that made it hard for me to not pounce on top of him. Then I slipped underneath the cool covers of his bed, intertwining his feet with mine as he reached over his nightstand to turn off the lights. Before I had a chance to say goodnight, I was blissfully falling asleep and snuggling next to the man I could now call mine.

16
Birthday Wrap-Up

As the quiet night turned into eye-squinting daylight, I awoke after barely getting a wink of sleep. Not because of Ozzy's stifled snoring or even because of Declan's brown noise app fogging the background. I was simply *happy*. And well, I didn't know what to do with myself. So I got up at the crack of dawn and treated myself to a breakfast snack of an Uncrustable peanut butter and jelly sandwich. He always had these in his fridge for those occasions when the cravings hit.

When Declan awoke an hour or so later, I heard him coming down the stairs, quickly approaching me at the kitchen table. "Good morning, honey," he said, planting a kiss on my lips. "How did you sleep?"

"Not too bad," I lied, trying to nonchalantly hide the fact that not only had I not slept well at all, I was still floating on air from the night before. Yup, I was still that silly 15-year-old school girl inside.

The weather was a cool 70 degrees without a drop of humidity, perfect for a stroll and moderate exercise at the nearby Kennesaw State Mountain Park. That same park Declan and I ended up stranded at during that heavy rainy downpour when we first met.

"I loved falling asleep next to you last night. Finally! I had you sleeping next to me," he said, pinching my butt.

"Silly! I loved it too. And I can tell you really love that brown noise app of yours."

"Did it bother you? I can turn it off tonight when we go to bed."

"No, babe. Not at all. You know I just like messing with ya."

"Alright, if you say so. Hey, honey – whaddaya say we start out our day by hiking up Kennesaw Mountain? Just like we did a couple of years ago. Get our blood flowing and all."

"Sounds fine by me. Let me just put on my gym clothes and we're out the door."

After changing into my new pair of criss-cross leggings, I grabbed two large bottles of water then met Declan in his garage. His car was already turned on, as he waited for me to get inside. I buckled up my seatbelt then placed my hand on his lap.

"Okay, babe. I'm ready!"

Seeing my cue that we were ready to go, Declan put on his Ray Ban shades that he kept on a car visor organizer meant for CDs, then backed up out into the driveway. The sun was slowly starting to rise, and soon we were driving off to meet her, while chasing deer I hoped I would actually see this time.

We decided not to err on the side of caution and took a different route I wasn't familiar with for our long hike once we arrived. Up and down trails and across various ponds, I followed Declan's lead. Even if not a single person seemed to be on the same path as us.

Soon we were hiking through overgrown bushes and too many rocks that were in the way, and as we did, Declan shared stories about almost every piece of historical artifact that surrounded us. "You see this log right here," he would say. "This is where the soldiers in the Civil War would take cover and hide. And this is where –"

His voice suddenly began to trail off. Or rather, I stopped paying attention. I couldn't care less about what happened in this battle, or what happened in that battle. My mind was tuned out, because I was enamored just being around my *boyfriend.*

Somehow or another, we ended up getting lost at one point. Right when we thought we were heading back toward the direction of his car, we suddenly found ourselves at an unrecognizable side of the park.

"Babe! We are going the wrong way! And to think you live here and I don't!" I joked.

"Geez. How did that happen?" he wondered. He looked so cute when confused. "Let me pull out my GPS. Okay, you're right. We gotta turn around. It'll only take eight hours if we decide to walk all the way home. You up for the challenge?" he winked.

"Yeah, okay, mista. I'll take your car and meet you at your place later today. Have fun! Don't mind me as I head on out!" I said, pretending to walk away.

"Ha ha. You think you're so funny, do ya, funny girl." His fingers poking me, almost knocking me into a pile of grassy weeds, I fell into a fit of giggles.

After we showered and freshened up back at the house late in the afternoon, it was time to get ready for the big-night, birthday celebration. I wanted to dress to impress for my man, so I put on my sexiest pair of heels and dolled up my face with volumizing mascara and a soft, smokey look around my green eyes. But, Declan, dressed to the nines, could have taken my breath away. Every time I looked at him, I fell in love with him more.

Bahama Breeze was his birthday dinner selection of choice. A live reggae band played nearby, as we sat at a booth facing each other close to a semi-closed off entryway. Feeling comforted by his presence, I reached over for Declan's hands and began stroking his thumb with mine. There was no strained look in his eyes anymore, and even some of the lines on his forehead started to disappear. After everything he had gone through these past couple of months, it was as if he was finally feeling like himself again. The only thing that mattered here and now was us, not doing anything else except simply *being* and *living.*

"Have you been having a good weekend so far?" I asked.

He nodded. "I really have. It's been great spending it with you and it's been a great birthday so far. And honey, I have to say, there is something I want to talk to you about."

"Yes?"

"Well, it's not a light subject matter but I feel it is something we can talk about now that we're together." His eyes suddenly turned serious.

"Sure, babe. I'm listening."

"Well, okay. I know how much you've said before that it means everything to you to have kids someday. I know your biggest dream is to become a mom. And I've never shared this with you before, but I did a vasectomy a few years ago when Bella's mom and I decided we didn't want any more kids."

"Why did you guys decide not to have any more kids after only having her?"

"Well, it's a story for another day but basically Bella's mom thought that due to my depression and hints of bipolar in the past, it just wouldn't be right."

"Bipolar disorder? I know we've talked about your mom possibly suffering from bipolar, but I've never seen you display any signs of bipolar disorder, babe."

"Yeah, I know you haven't. But I digress. That's not the point I wanted to get at. My point is, even though I did a vasectomy a few years ago, I would reverse it. I would totally do it for you. You're the only woman I would ever do it for. Not ex wife number two, not anyone. Just you."

"Thanks, love. That's sweet. Means everything to me to hear you say that."

"There's something else, too."

"Oh?" I wasn't quite sure if I should be concerned or anxious to hear more.

"Okay, sooooo. I just know that you and I would have a boy," he said, with a smile so wide you would have thought I had just announced I was pregnant. "As a matter of fact, I'm certain of it."

"You're so silly," I smiled, now giving him my full attention. Declan's random thoughts were on full spring again, and it was one of the reasons I loved him so. "What makes you say that, babe?"

"I feel it. I feel like God would want me to have a boy so I could raise him to be a good man. Annnnndddd he would have your green eyes. He would be a Brazilian-American-Spaniard. Imagine that. He would be the ultimate chic magnet!"

I laughed. Here Declan was, already predicting our future and the type of child we would have, something only women ordinarily did. *How did I get so lucky.*

Off to the corner, a group of teenagers was singing *happy birthday* to young girl with a hip-hugging skirt and long, dangling hoop earrings, sitting two tables down from ours. And the band, sporting their Hawaiian shirts, momentarily stopped playing, leaving a CD blasting on loop to entertain the audience. Declan's voice grew softer now, as he looked at me with deep set love in his eyes.

"Honey, you always do things from the heart," he noted. His voice sounded sincere and steady, as he looked at me from across the booth. "You took massive risks with me, even with the possibility of no rewards. I love you for it even though I don't understand it myself. So you know I have to ask. What made you always think we were a good match?"

I could tell he was probably questioning what I *ever* saw in him. Out of all the men, *why him.* Why, then; and why, now. But the answer to me was simple.

"Sweetie," I said, trying to tune out the distracting sounds of the teenagers around us. "I have always felt like I've known your heart and soul. When we met two years ago, you were the first person in a very long time that made me feel alive. I didn't think you'd be back in my life, but I knew then you were the only one for me. And this year, by the grace of God, even in this short time, even in the middle of so much chaos, I've seen you transform. I've seen the kind of man you want to be. And the connection we share has always…. but I mean *always* run deep."

With the palm of Declan's hand in mine, my thumb began to trickle down the outer lines of his fingertips when I heard a sniffle. I looked up and noticed surprising tears form in his eyes. He didn't have to say a word. The love and sorrow that carried him all these years was here equally my own.

Upon wrapping up dinner at Bahama Breeze, Declan and I took it upon ourselves to just enjoy the remainder of the night in the cozy confines of his inviting bedroom. Who said these two adults had to stay out late like the rest of them?

Still in mid-August, the heat outside was enough to make us feel a bit too warm for our liking, even if we were in a cool 70-degree, air-conditioned room with silk curtains drawn.

Declan had already taken to it to remove his tight-fitting white t-shirt, revealing his flat and shaven stomach that looked as smooth as a baby's bottom. I could feel myself suddenly desiring to have him close, perhaps too close, and even inside me. And even though we hadn't revisited his celibacy talk now that we were official, I imagined nothing of it had changed.

I was sitting on Declan's bed, with a pillow propped up behind my back, just admiring his physique when I suddenly felt an intense headache come plunging at me full force. "Fuck! Fuck! This hurts!" I whined. I didn't care if I sounded like a complete baby at the mercy of this nagging, stupid headache.

"What's going on, hun?" Declan was now on the foot of the bed, facing me concerned, with his t-shirt nowhere in sight.

"I don't know… I suddenly got this damn headache and it's killing me!"

"Do you need me to get you anything? Maybe some Advil?"

"No, it's okay, babe. You don't have to."

"I know I don't have to but I'm going to anyway. And when I come back, you better give me the best head of my life!" he smirked. Even in my agonizing pain, I wondered if he had just said what I thought he did. *Mr. So-Called Celibate Man wanted me to go down on him? Was the Advil messing with my head and making me hear things?*

It seemed like no time had passed at all when Declan approached me with two Advils and a glass of cold water in the cup of his hand. "If this doesn't work, honey, I'll just have to spank your ass and that will make your headache go away in a heartbeat."

And just like that, between two Advils down my throat and Declan beckoning to have his way with me, I was no longer thinking about my headache. No, what my mind was suddenly preoccupied with was taking advantage of this fun and flirtatious mood *my man* was in and not letting it go to waste. So I crawled my body next to Declan in bed, removed my sleeveless top to expose my bra, and began massaging his upper thigh. "You don't need to spank my ass," I said. "We can save that for later. My headache is gone now anyway. But I know what else we can do..."

I could feel Declan's body slowly inch toward mine, not even hesitating for a second as I saw a bulge rise underneath his shorts. I quietly asked if I could continue, and when he responded that he wanted to already have himself inside me, I knew he didn't have to say anything more. From his upper thigh to over his waist, I started to gently move my hand toward his shaft, as his breath accelerated with mine. And when he gasped as I moved my tongue up and down, and bobbed my head to the side, I knew there was suddenly no turning back.

"Babe, I'm about to – I'm about to –" he muttered in half breaths, until suddenly I felt his body push itself away. I wanted to tell him to relax, to remind him that it was okay.

"Babe, I can't do this," he finally said. He was now trying to position himself straight up on the headboard as his eyes began to water. "I'm so sorry – I want to so badly, but I feel some blockage of some sort that prevents me from letting go. I guess I'm still emotionally traumatized."

"I don't want to make you uncomfortable, so it's okay if you want to stop," I said, trying my best to cover up my now-raging hormones. Even if I was deeply frustrated, I couldn't dare let it show. I wanted Declan to feel safe with me and to lose control with me in every way, but I didn't know what it would take to get there. So in the end, hot and heavy, just as the heat outside with nothing to provide it relief, is how we, too, fell asleep that night.

I arose Sunday morning with Declan once again sleeping quietly beside me, as if there was no lingering sexual frustration from the night before. And although I still hadn't gotten used to the fact that we were now sleeping on the same bed, it was a strange feeling to know that all we did was *literally* sleep on the same bed, and nothing more.

Not one to hide any twinge of jealousy, Ozzy was comfortably resting at the foot of our legs, watching us. Any slight movement that led him to believe we would awaken each other with a kiss or a playful touch underneath the sheets, he was ready to step between and separate.

When Declan awoke, he turned over to my side of the bed and apologized about the night before.

"Hey hun. About last night – I don't even know what to say about it," he began. "I just want you to know that was a mistake."

A mistake? Trying to be intimate with the woman he loved was a mistake? I was confused and didn't understand – while Declan had no problem talking dirty with me, now any sexual advances between us came with a *no bueno* sign. Although one minute he would imply that he wanted to have his way with me, the next minute the thought of seducing me (or me seducing him) was off limits and foreign.

"What do you mean last night was a mistake?" I asked, trying to make sure I remained calm and level-headed with my tone.

"I love you but I just need to stick to my celibacy promise, that's all. I'm clearly not ready to be intimate after all I've been through and go down that path."

"Umm, okay," I muttered, saying no more. I was starting to get mixed signals about where we stood in the bedroom department, but I realized probing the matter any further wouldn't do us any good. This was our time together, and whatever made Declan feel comfortable and safe, is the commitment I was still sticking to.

Only five minutes on Barrett Knoll Parkway was a church called North Metro that Declan had taken a recent liking to. Even before dinner at Bahama Breeze the night before, we had planned to wake up Sunday morning and check out one of the two services offered that day. While I personally enjoyed arriving to church extra early in order to worship and sing with the band, Declan could have done without all the "unnecessary hoopla" as he liked to call it.

"They play for too long. 25 minutes is just too long," he griped, as we discussed whether to attend the first or second morning service after we both got up from bed.

By the time we made our way around to the already crowded parking lot for the 11 a.m. service, swarms of people were scattered at a small food stand by the front, grabbing a late-morning cup of coffee before entering the auditorium.

Not wanting to stay downstairs for the band, Declan and I walked up a flight of stairs to the overflow room instead and sat in the back, close to another couple that took up their seats next to us. Only a dozen or so people sat in our general vicinity. Declan never liked to be the center of attention nor was he the kind to make a spectacle of things.

"All things are working for my good because He's intentional, never failing. I don't have to worry about anything, because He's working for him."

161

The worship band was nearing the end of their last song of a four-song opening playlist. I could smell Declan's cologne rubbing off my ruffled up quarter-sleeve top as I nuzzled my head on his neck.

"We made it just in time for the service, hun," he whispered, putting his arm over my shoulder and his feet underneath his chair. "I'm so glad we're getting to experience going to church together again."

"This church looks really neat. I know you were having a hard time going to Buckhead, being so far away from you and all, so I'm glad you found this place, babe." Before I could go on, the backstage lights on the stage started to dim, as the pastor entered to speak and we fixated our eyes to watch him on the big screen.

"Good morning, everyone! Welcome! We are so happy to have you here with us at North Metro today. If it is your first time here, welcome, welcome!"

As the service began, Declan and I listened intently as the pastor raised his voice in a jubilant tone that echoed across all corners of the church and settled back to his lips. I'd be lying if I said I remember what his faith-based message was that day. Because even as I tried to pay attention and set my eyes on the words of wisdom that were being bestowed upon me, all I could think about were my special moments with Declan on this trip. There was no denying that each detail and each moment had led me here, to this moment where we could hold hands at church as a demonstration of our growing love and dedication to one another. Even as Declan sometimes struggled on knowing what to do.

I closed my eyes and praised God for this moment, for allowing me to experience His everlasting glory these past couple of days with Declan. *I would have never thought two years ago that I would be back here someday. Thank you, Jesus. Thank you for opening up our hearts and showing the way. Thank you for everything.*

I wasn't ready to fly back home. I didn't want to wake up from this dream that changed everything for me. Because it was a dream. It was every bit of a dream turned reality, the kind you envision and cling onto so tightly as a young girl yet never possibly think will actually happen to you. Because why would it. Why should you think yourself capable of seeing your wildest dreams come true. Why should you believe that you are capable of being with the man you've always loved. Why should you believe that love, in every way, could be yours. But it was – and it was more than mine. It was everything that was meant to be mine before I even knew it myself.

Together, Declan and I had found a way back to each other that not even the most well-renowned psychics could have predicted. I wanted to stay here, staring into his eyes and allowing myself to be part of this sweet symphony. He was everything I wanted and everything I never thought I'd have.

9:01 p.m. Journal Entry–

It's been almost a full week since everything so beautifully changed. I still can't believe it. I still can't believe that he chose me. I still can't get over how often he tells me he loves me, and every time it's as if it's the first time. It's such a dream and more than everything I ever wanted. "It's not a dream," my friend reminded me. "It's reality." I'm trying to take in every moment. To tell myself that I, too, deserve this. That I, too, deserve to be happy. In the words of one of my favorite songs, I'm a lover of his presence and I was made for loving him.

PART V –

Changes

"Deep within I'm shaken by the
violence of existing for only you."

— *Sarah McLachlan*

17

Oregon

A couple of weeks after I returned to South Florida, I packed my bags again to head to the most Pacific Northwest parts of the country: Portland, Oregon. Earlier in the year, long before Declan and I reconnected, I started to feel myself getting bit by the traveling bug. Try as I did, it was a feeling I couldn't shake off. And although I made it a point to schedule international trips on a regular yearly basis, I soon realized I wasn't exploring the great wonders of what lied right here at home.

"Take advantage to travel as much as you can while you don't have kids." My dad's voice and nuggets of wisdom seemed to once again echo inside my head.

Brian, a dear friend of mine who lived outside of Portland, often tried to convince me to make the journey to see this enticing, coastal state that many did not know much about. Except to say that people there ventured more on the *kooky* side and firmly stood by the motto *live and let live.* Or perhaps to put it more accurately: *Live wildly and let others live wildly, too.*

"I know you would simply fall in love in Oregon," Brian would say every time I mentioned how much I wanted to travel and escape. Anywhere away from Florida was good enough for me.

So why not kill two birds with one stone, and not only enjoy nature-filled adventures with my friend, but also take some time out to explore a state I knew would be entirely different from anywhere I had ever been to? I'd be a fool not to.

My flight was booked. I'd fly out Labor Day weekend.

Declan knew about my summer itinerary that I pre-programmed months in advance. "Go and have fun, honey. Make the best of it. I love you," he texted me on my connecting flight out of Texas.

What felt like 10 hours later but was more like five hours, I landed in Portland.

Decked out in a pair of casual shorts and a lightweight Hawaiian shirt perfect for the summer, Brian smiled excitedly as he and his college-bound daughter waited to greet me at the front of the Portland International airport. It was my first time meeting one of his daughters, though I had already known Brian for several years.

A multiple-marathon runner and passionate athlete, Brian and I connected through an LA Fitness page on Facebook. He was a gym cycling instructor, and I had dabbled with the idea of getting spinning certification myself. It had not been that long ago since he visited Miami with his teenage son, and we were sampling delicious dinner entrees and desserts at a popular restaurant in town; and now in exchange, Brian and his family were my gracious hosts in Oregon.

Prior to my trip, Brian asked me to make note of any famous attraction I wanted to see or any place in particular I wanted to go to. With a long weekend ahead of us, he would do what he could to squeeze them in.

"Welllll….." I said, "I've always wanted to see a waterfall, and Cheryl Strayed's book *Wild* is one of my favorites. She lost her mother like I did, and she had a couple of really devastating and heartbreaking relationships with men. I read her book in one sitting and cried the whole way through.

"I know she lives here in Portland, and her book is based on her story of hiking the Pacific Crest Trail in order to find herself again. I've always found it fascinating to hear how much the PCT changed her. I would love to step foot on it, if possible. Just to be where she once was."

As we stepped outside the airport late that afternoon, a cool breeze swept over my face, and I inhaled what felt like the purest form of fresh air. I was dumbfounded. There was simply no humidity here. *Yup, I was definitely not in South Florida anymore.* Loading my bags into Brian's SUV, a *"Welcome to Portland"* sign hanging overhead swayed back and forth in the wind. I couldn't wait to see what plans Brian had up his sleeve.

Pittock Mansion. Silver Falls State Park. Multnomah Falls. Columbia River Gorge. Mount Hood. Downtown Portland. McMenanims. Even karaoke at an off-beat bar. There was almost nothing that Brian didn't have on the agenda for us during my short stay, and somehow, we did them all.

I almost squealed like a little school girl when I heard the crashing roar of a waterfall on our first day out and about. I jumped up and down when I purchased a pre-signed copy of one of Cheryl Strayed's books at a local bookstore. I delighted at the sweet taste of freshly-grown concord grapes from Brian's very own backyard vineyard. And I marveled at the breathtaking sight of Mount Hood, one of the most famous volcanoes in the northern part of Oregon that looks like a picture-perfect postcard by anybody who steps into its view.

Not too far of a drive from Mount Hood was Timberline Lodge, a ski resort that is famously known as one of the filming locations for *The Shining*. Considered a national historic landmark, Timberline Lodge stands 60 miles or so outside of Portland.

It was my second-to-last day in Oregon, and Brian and I, along with his wife, Jill, and teenage son, Reed, spent the entire morning and afternoon hiking up steep hills and mountainous terrain that led to the most stunning waterfalls. I had not exercised for days, and with so much walking up and down and climbing up and down, I started feeling pretty spent. But Brian insisted we make one final adventure out of our day and check out this winter wonderland lodge, off to the south side of Mount Hood.

After getting an exclusive tour inside Timberline Lodge – seeing replica rooms of where former U.S. presidents once stayed – we stepped out onto a balcony, to a spectacular panoramic view, overlooking the natural beauty of Oregon. Snow set on mountain tops and a chill in the air felt comforting. *It couldn't get much better than this.*

Both Brian's wife and son then ventured off to relax in a couple of patio chairs by a free-for-all gaming area outside. While one tourist man played *Jenga,* his child fidgeted with loose marbles inside a scrunched-up, clear bag that looked completely worn. I was about to sit down myself and take a breather when Brian stopped me.

"Nope, there is one more thing I want you to see."

"Briaaaan, I'm tired. We've been walking all day. I don't think I can walk anymore," I grumbled, tugging on my shirt like a child.

"Yes, you can. Of course you can. C'mon. One more thing. Let's gooo," he waved, as he started up a hill.

I begrudgingly followed, trying to pick up my pace as I looked up and saw him twenty feet or so ahead of me. The long, steep hill that stood adjacent to Timberline Lodge made my legs want to give out with every move. But up we went, and up we hiked. After a good 10-minute walk, Brian turned around and faced me, patiently waiting for me to catch up to him. We were on top of the hill now and a vast nature trail surrounded us. Several trees were bare, with nothing but their roots reaching out into the sky, while other branches remained full and lush. Mount Hood stood tall, far off in the distance, its volcanic gas emitting slowly in the air. Not a single cloud was within sight. And the sky was as blue as I remembered my mother's eyes.

"Do you know where you are?" asked Brian.

"Umm... on top of a hill?" I responded.

"Yes and no," he said, pointing at a sign behind me. "Turn around..."

I looked across my shoulder and saw a marker sign pinned down to a weathered post on the ground: *Pacific Crest National Scenic Trail – Canada 550 miles/ Mexico 2108 miles*

I was standing on the Pacific Crest Trail.

On the exact same spot of the trail that one of my favorite authors trekked for 94 days. Memories of reading *Wild* on an eight-hour flight home from Brazil flashed before me. Of a book that changed me, much like I imagined the PCT changed Cheryl Strayed. In this infinite space and time, I suddenly felt connected to her. To all her heartache. To all her pain. To those moments when she wondered if her life was in vain. Here I was, in the presence of a divine universal power, living and breathing a full circle moment. I couldn't help but fall to my knees and cry.

Seeing me overcome with emotion and needing some time on my own, Brian extended his arm around me then told me he would meet me at the bottom of the hill when I was ready. "Take all the time you need," he said.

My eyes darted toward the sky and a streak of clouds began to appear. I looked around, observing the soft sounds and sights of nature standing before me and taking its graceful bow. I could see large footprints in the dirt sand of hikers who once walked through here.

Boulder-sized field rocks were spread throughout different parts of the trail, and little patches of green poked out of indistinguishable bushes. I picked up a few laying pebbles and held them in my hands, allowing the small particles of dust to fall through my fingers.

I thought of my mother, how much I missed her so. And I remembered how much pain I was in when I read *Wild*. It was almost a year ago, and I was returning home to Florida after spending the holidays with my family in Brazil. One of my twin cousins was recently married, and the other one was recently engaged. Everybody around me was happy. Everybody except me.

It had been a long time since I was in a fulfilling relationship, and I wondered if I would ever find love again. But not just any love. *Real love.* The love that strips you down to the bone and reveals a side of you that you didn't know yourself.

I thought about Declan, and how I could never have expected he would come into my life again. I wondered if my mother would have liked him, if she would have embraced him just as much as I did. So I wept. Not because I was in any pain, *no*. But because for the first time in a very long time I was happy. I was truly just… *happy*.

And then, as I gazed toward the blue horizon, it came to me. A feeling so strong, so powerful, I could have sworn God was standing right next to me and whispering into my ear.

It is time for you to move on and turn the page to a new chapter in your life. Your time in Florida is done. You've been there for your father in his time of need, and you were there for your mother when she was still on Earth. But there is nothing else for you to do at home. Florida no longer serves you nor can it do anything else for you. That chapter is closed. Your life now awaits you in Georgia. Be bold and take that step when the time comes.

I can only recall maybe one or two other occasions when I felt myself face-to-face with an epiphany that was so vividly clear, it left me awestruck. I didn't know when or how it would come to be – all I knew is that I would soon move to Georgia, because a force, greater than myself, was telling me so.

Standing on the Pacific Crest Trail the only thing that mattered was that I understood. Soon, this turning point in my life would require me to be fearless and unafraid.

18

Scotch in Georgia

My trip to Oregon exceeded all of my expectations, and then some. Breathtakingly beautiful, it quickly moved to the top of my list of favorite states in the country, coveting the number two spot. After Georgia, of course.

After stepping foot on the Pacific Crest Trail, I confided in only four people the epiphany I had: my dad, my best friend Oceana, Brian and Declan. And as our relationship continued to blossom, Declan insisted that I take the next step and move to Georgia, like, now.

"I still think you should just move up here and live with me – just saying. We can figure out the whole job thing later," he said one morning, as I was still trying to wake up during my long commute to work.

Now that we were seriously dating, there was no question that eventually I'd have to take the plunge and uproot my life to the Peach State. In exactly a year my lease would be up, and so we agreed I'd pack up my belongings (with my dog Lumee in tow) and move then. That seemed like the logical answer.

And though we began to slowly discuss what our future entailed together (*Would we have a joint bank account? Or separate? Would we move out of his God-forsaken house that had been nothing but a curse with ex #2 and into a home we could call our own? How would Lumee and Ozzy get along?*), I was firm on one request: I had to meet Bella before we ever truly considered my moving.

Because I was around her age myself when my own parents divorced, it was important to me that she was given the space and time necessary to get to know me and feel comfortable around me. But there was too much still going on in Declan's life, and it was still much too soon to even really approach the subject of how I would meet her, much less be introduced to her. We'd talk about it again at a later date.

Since Declan is, as he would describe it, a loner, with only a select few number of friends, I was never really introduced to anybody in his inner circle. But one person knew about me, and she had known about me ever since John passed, when I was by Declan's side in Melbourne. Or maybe she knew about me even sooner.

I met his friend Caren the weekend after Labor Day, when I was in Georgia yet again, for the umpteenth time. It had become a running joke at this point with my friends at home that I was more *there* than I ever was *here*. A curly-haired married woman in her thirties, Caren worked as a veterinarian on the outskirts of Kennesaw. The fact that she was a huge animal lover like myself was a big plus.

Caren and her husband were the only people, aside from myself, who were fully aware of Declan's recent troubles, including his undeniably messy divorce. It was a Saturday around lunchtime when we walked into her office with Ozzy, who was overdue on his semi-annual shots.

Unable to sit still, Ozzy fumbled around the immaculately clean veterinarian office, as Caren almost tripped over him, trying to make her way across the room.

"Hi there! You must be Maíra. Nice to meet you. I've heard so much about you. I'm Caren," she said, reaching out her hand and flashing a welcoming smile. Even in her spotless professional attire, she exuded warmth and kindness.

After a bit of small talk, it was time for Ozzy to be ushered into the back room for his shots. Ten minutes later, Caren came out to tell Declan and

I that everything was good to go. She then asked if she could speak to me briefly in private.

"Sure," I said, before letting Declan know I would be right back. Once out in the hallway, Caren grabbed my hand and looked at me with a gentle smile.

"Thanks for taking care of Ozzy," I said, wanting to break the ice and keep our conversation smooth and friendly.

"No, thank you for everything you've done for him," she said, looking back inside the vet examination room, where Declan now sat browsing through his phone. "Even in his dark days, thanks for being there, as I'm sure it hasn't been all that easy when his mood swings take center stage and he's sometimes a difficult person to love."

This was the second time someone had brought up to me the notion of so-called mood swings. Apparently it was known to a few others except myself that Declan was prone to change his character, and venture off into a dark abyss I still knew nothing about. I knew Declan still struggled with the recent divorce and his brother's passing, but he had never given me any inclination of anything for me to be particularly concerned about. So, just as I had done with Daisy, I shrugged off Caren's words to mean nothing.

Later in the afternoon, Declan mentioned that he had to step out for a while to attend his daughter's last cheerleading practice of the season. Not a problem, I told him, I would stay behind tending to Ozzy, who was already zoning out after his set of shots.

"Really?" he said, "You don't mind that I have to go? I'm surprised you're not mad at me."

"Why would I be mad?"

"I don't know," he shrugged. "It's just that the *other one* would have gotten in an argument with me about it."

"I'm not your ex-wife #2," I firmly yet playfully reminded him.

From rushing Ozzy to the vet to Bella's longer-than-expected cheerleading practice, Declan looked tired and beat once he was back home. With my now general routine of resting my head on his chest, we cozied up together on the couch, and began watching a World War II documentary that played on Netflix. Anything that could make us forget a bit about our own lives. I couldn't stay long in Georgia this time around. The very next day, Declan would take me to the airport again so I could get ready for work the coming week.

While Declan seemed deeply entranced by talks of bombing and Hitler and Pearl Harbor, I was less than amused and soon my stomach started to grumble. Rushing back and forth between different places all day long left us with no time to grab a bite to eat.

"Babe, would you mind if we get some dinner when the documentary is over? I don't know if you've noticed but we haven't eaten all day."

"How about we go now? I'm getting hungry myself. I can catch up on this later," he said, turning off his HDTV and grabbing his car keys. "Let me just run upstairs real quick to change and then we're out."

If there is one thing I loved to eat in Georgia it was their mac and cheese. But not just any mac and cheese – no. The most delicious, cheesy mac and cheese could only be found at a fancy-schmancy place called *Aspens Signature Steakhouse,* right in the heart of Marietta. And while many people were there for the filet mignon with a bourbon glaze, I only wanted my mouth-watering, five-cheese mac and cheese. With a sprinkle of parmesan on top. So off we went.

Aspens Signature Steakhouse made you feel like you were just checking in to your reservation at a rustic lodging. Adorned with high ceilings and warm glowing lanterns on every table, its cozy environment inside was not only inviting but it was beautiful too. Although people were typically known to have dinner into the late hours of the night at this upscale restaurant, Declan and I decided we would just grab a couple of appetizers and drinks at the bar instead.

Looking sophisticated and sexy with his long-sleeved, buttoned-down shirt, Declan appeared like he belonged here. After ordering an appetizer portion of their famous mac and cheese, along with a couple of refreshing cocktails that we downed in a matter of minutes, our server, a Georgia native dressed to the nines, came up to us and noted how happy we looked.

"Pardon me but I have to ask. Are you guys dating or just friends?"

Tapping my thigh, Declan glanced at me then smiled. "She's my girlfriend."

It was the first time he had introduced us with an official title in public, and though little things like this wouldn't make much of a difference to anyone else, to me, having Declan regard me as *the* one and only woman by his side was just beyond special. Behind my sour apple martini, I wondered if anybody could see me blush.

After finishing our cocktails, we agreed to stop at Publix next to pick up some Merlot wine *(what else?)* then head back to Declan's place to continue our own little party in our favorite spot: his living room. In between our chats about our not-too-far-off future and me eventually meeting his daughter, Declan would stop me mid-conversation and surprise me with a kiss. "You have such soft lips, babe."

We were still both floating on cloud nine, so to speak, and every minute spent together was another minute of a natural high neither of us wanted to get down from. And then it got dark. *Really dark.* To this day I almost can't explain it.

Declan and I were one minute stealing kisses from each other and engaging in deep conversation like we typically always do, to the next, Declan was in tears and rocking his body in the fetal position on the floor. I had literally turned my head away for what seemed like only a split second to grab some juice from the kitchen counter, to then find Declan downing one too many glasses of wine and one too many sips of scotch whiskey. Not one to ever mix drinks, there he lay, belligerent and out of touch, almost asking someone to hold him. I suddenly didn't recognize him and I suddenly didn't know what the hell was going on. And somewhere deep inside, dare I say I was even a bit scared.

The alcohol was triggering a deep-rooted depression, one I had only suspected to a certain extent in past months, given the overwhelming nature of everything he had to overcome, and was still overcoming. But now, it was fast bubbling its way up to the surface. Now here, vulnerable and unguarded, Declan's deepest fears started to show. And I was starting to believe there was something even deeper here. Something I didn't even know.

I had never seen Declan this way. His eyes, red-stricken with tears; just looking at me, as if there was nothing anybody could do for him. He murmured how much he would hurt anybody who tried to hurt him. He mentioned the divorce and he mentioned his brother. But none of it made sense. By now, Declan was shaking. There was no consoling him. Back and forth, back and forth. He continued to rock and sway as if he couldn't acknowledge my presence here beside him.

Tremendous grief and pain still consumed his entire being, and I was helpless, cradling a man who looked at me like a wounded bear lost in the woods.

"Who are you?" His red-shot eyes suddenly darted straight at me, so dark and piercing it made me take a step back.

"Honey, it's me. It's Maíra. You're safe, babe. You're here with me."

"Somebody is trying to hurt me!" he screamed. "Get them away! I will hurt anybody who tries to hurt me!"

Declan was at the verge of becoming incoherent, and while under the effects of alcohol, I didn't know if he was capable of getting up and breaking any object that stood in his way, or lashing out at me by mistaking me with someone else. Whether it was his ex #2 or somebody else. Stunned and speechless, I didn't know what to do. I was at a loss for words.

Even though I had no way of knowing what was going on inside his brain, or what was causing such emotional havoc from within, one thing was certain: I couldn't leave him to fall asleep on the cold living room floor. He was almost shivering now, and twenty minutes into this unexplainable episode, he was rocking still. This time, almost violently.

Double my size, I also knew there was no way I could carry Declan on my own to the bedroom. So instead I tried to gently convince him that down here, both literally and metaphorically speaking, was nowhere to be.

"Honey, it's okay…" I whispered. "It's okay, my love. I'm here. You're not alone, sweetie. I promise you that you're not. Let me help you to bed. I'll stay right here with you. Will you let me help you to bed, please?"

I put my hand on his shoulder and offered him a glass of water, hoping it would calm him but he refused.

"No!" he barked. "Get that away from me! Where am I? Where am I??"

I couldn't believe what I was hearing, what I was seeing – what I was witnessing in and all around me. Not only did it seem like he didn't recognize me, he could no longer even register that he was in the comfort of his own home. Without any clear explanation, it was as if Declan had completely lost touch with reality, and I was there left to figure out a way to pull him away from all the madness.

Noticing my cell phone still on top of the coffee table next to us, I grabbed it and texted my friend Angie, hoping to gods of all gods she was still awake.

"Angie, it's me. Please tell me you're there. There's something going on with Declan and I don't know what. I think he had too much to drink tonight and he's acting crazy. Not like himself at all. I'm trying to calm him down. But I don't know what the fuck to do!"

"Are you safe?? Where are you?"

"I'm totally safe. I'm at his house. I just don't know how to get him to snap out of this. He's talking crazy shit. He doesn't even recognize me! What do I do?!"

"Give him water. Give him food. Try to take him to his bedroom so he can sleep it off. He may be exhibiting signs of bipolar or depression. Alcohol only makes it 10x worse. Are you sure you're okay? Do you know any of his neighbors?"

"I'm okay. I've just never seen him like this. It's blowing my mind! Okay, I'll do what you said. Thank you. Love you."

"Love you too. I'll be right here. I'm not going to sleep until you tell me everything is okay and you're going to sleep yourself."

Approaching Declan ever so gently, I offered to give him water once more. After refusing to drink it at first, he then took two full sips, one gulp after another. By some miracle of God, I somehow then managed to get Declan upstairs and soon he was fast asleep, with Ozzy on the foot of the bed, duvet covers up to his neck – and me wondering what the hell just happened. He was quiet and motionless now, sleeping blissfully like a baby. You would have never guessed that just a few minutes before Dr. Jekyl and Mr. Hyde were in the room, trying to make our acquaintance.

It was then I began to fully realize how much Declan was truly trauma- tized by everything still, and in all likelihood, just starting to feel the lingering effects of post-traumatic stress and – at the very least – an unforgiving depres- sion that had its claws on him now, and was unwilling to let go.

The next day, when Declan awoke, he was unable to recall a single thing that happened the night before. He could not remember when I covered him with multiple blankets in bed and placed another glass of water on his nightstand, nor could he remember his uncontrollable sobs as I tried to rub his back and soothe him. The only thing he could remember was us chatting outside in the patio, before heading back into the living room, daydreaming and fantasizing about glimpses into our future. But he could remember noth- ing that transpired when we were back inside his house.

"I'm sorry I got that way and you saw me like that. I didn't mean to scare you. I can't remember a thing…" he said, kissing me on the forehead after grabbing a gallon of water from the kitchen. "It will never happen again, I promise."

"No need to apologize, honey. I think you probably just had a bit too much to drink and were in pain. It's okay. We've all been there," I reassured him, trying hard not to let show how terrified I had actually been.

I wasn't about to point the finger and start judging Declan because of what one could chop off to a single night of too much scotch. Or was alcohol really to blame here? I had never seen this side to Declan before and I wondered if I should be concerned. And even though I knew I didn't have the answers, one thing was quickly becoming clear: The road to healing would be long, and it would be more emotionally taxing than I could have ever imagined.

8:22 p.m. Journal Entry –

To say the last 24 hours have been interesting and unexpected would be an understatement. I hurt for Declan and I wish I could take his pain and make it entirely my own. Before he took me to the airport today, we spent the day just taking it easy after the crazy alcohol episode of last night. Last night was rough. I left a letter for him in his bathroom this afternoon. I wanted to remind him how much I love him, and how I will be right by his side through it all, through the good days and not-so-good days. I started to cry when he dropped me off at the airport. For the first time, it was really hard for me to say goodbye, and for some reason, I struggled leaving him. I never want to leave him and I hate that I have no other choice.

19

Twisted by Depression

"**H**ey, wyd?"

As if overnight, Declan's demeanor drastically started to change, and the extent of our conversations became limited to two-word sentences and abbreviations transmitted via text in a 24-hour time frame. Ever so slowly yet suddenly, his words of tender affection and concern began to evaporate into thin air. A typical "How was your day, honey?" now turned into "Hey, wyd?" without a second thought.

Gone were the days of long, late-night chats over the phone. He was now simply *distant.* I worried we would have a repeat from two years ago and he would disappear again. And since my last visit to Georgia, I worried that this re-appearing depression would pull him away.

From the time we first met, Declan considered himself to legitimately suffer from bipolar disorder, something he had no issue revealing to me. Over the years, however, Declan came to be officially diagnosed with chronic depression by his psychiatrist (even though I always thought it to be more of a combination of the two).

It was only in his early twenties that Declan experienced his first depressive episode, as the result of severe drug usage at the University of Florida in Gainesville. There, he admits, life consisted of an assortment of hallucinating, flying colors and every drug under the sun. And it was this drug abuse – along with the history of mental illness on his mother's side of the family – that would later lead to an ongoing state of depression for the greater portion of his life, as well as generate shattering consequences in his romantic relationships.

I knew when Declan was in a depressed frame of mind. He retreated and bottled himself up whole. While encouraging him to express his emotions worked in the past, such as when we first started to reconnect earlier in the year, now any attempts and efforts to talk to him proved futile and of no use. The more space I gave Declan to deal with his own negative self-talk on his own, the better. I also knew when he was out of the depression and back to acting like himself. Not only would he distinctly say so (*"I'm no longer depressed today, and it's such a relief"*), but he would also show concern and act loving again (*"Hey honey. I wanna hear how your day went today. I really miss you, by the way."*)

One time, Declan described being depressed as not just a matter of being "blah," but as something much deeper than that. It was about mustering enough energy to be a serviceable human being throughout the day, just enough to get you to the night, when you no longer felt like you have to hide from the torment inside your head. But then you get to a point where you don't have the mental stamina to continue the battle against it. Simply put, it's "exhausting," he would say.

I knew that just when he thought he had time to start processing the traumatic events from earlier in the year, another crisis would occur, and this is what left him feeling drained, day in and day out. Almost inevitably, Declan's mood swings gradually increased, and though I was just living a dream a few weeks prior up with him in Georgia, now I was holding onto the bar handles of the rollercoaster ride of depression, not knowing which sharp turn it would take or where we would ultimately end up.

And so I began to turn to God again, asking Him to please keep his purpose for my relationship with Declan in place, even when the difficult moments came. And when I began to feel isolated, I turned to my journal and wrote entry upon entry, sometimes multiple times in one day, since I couldn't tell my own boyfriend how I was feeling. *He will shut me out. He's going through his own stuff.*

There was only one person I could completely open up my heart to: my father. I invited him over for coffee one late September afternoon, a couple of weeks after returning home from that drunken episode I wish I could forget. As he often did, dad walked in with a grocery plastic bag in hand and some savory treats – Cuban ham croquettes (my favorite) and cream cheese-filled pastries.

Ever since I was a little girl, I looked up to my father as my hero. I saw the devastation the divorce with my mother caused him over the years, and I saw what a terrible fit his second wife was for him from the moment we met. In many ways, I also saw my father in Declan; they were more similar than they were different.

I looked to my father as my hero not only for his sheer strength to overcome broken marriages, but also for his relentless willpower to fight a horrible disease. In 2008, after experiencing severe stomach pain, a doctor pulled my father into his office to deliver the God-awful news: *You have ------.* Yup, that six-letter word I refuse to utter to this day. And to make matters worse, it was stage 4. Right as dad was getting ready to retire, right as dad was in the process of publishing his first non-fiction book *(it runs in the family...)*. Pure shock and devastation wouldn't even begin to describe it.

The dreaded phone call of his diagnosis that brought me to my knees happened while I was at work. I couldn't imagine the thought of losing my father, the man who was there for me through thick and thin. My biggest fan and my biggest supporter of all decisions I made in my life, even if he didn't always agree with them. Even if it meant flying to Georgia again and again, in search of holding onto the one thing I felt was right: my soulmate.

With countless number of chemo sessions under his belt, and against all medical odds and expectations, dad continues to fight the good fight – even a decade later. It was his steadfast strength and quiet wisdom I appreciated the most every time we hung out together, just as he poured himself a hot cup of coffee in my kitchen that Saturday afternoon.

Lumee loved it every time *abuelo* came over and picked him up over his shoulder. Dad's hair was thinning now, and he looked tired after taking another round of drug cocktails to keep his condition at bay. But Lumee was always excited to see him, and he had no problem making it known as he ran little licking laps across dad's face.

Although I am one to often share everything with my father, I felt protective about mine and Declan's relationship. Distressed and alone, I needed Declan's love but I didn't want dad to see that I was hurting. But dad knew better — he could tell something was up – when he pulled his chair next to mine at the kitchen table, and Lumee lay down beside us to take a nap. He could see it in my eyes.

"*Filha,* if I may. Let me just say one thing to you. In all my sixty-something years of walking this Earth, I can say this much: When a man loves a woman, he will do everything for her, and more. He will go to the ends of the planet and back."

He grabbed my hand as I meekly kept my eyes lowered to the ground, watching Lumee's soft breathing almost turn into a cat's purr, his little tummy vibrating up and down.

"I know, dad… I know," I responded. "My love for Declan is endless and limitless, but I know I need to be good to me, too. It pains me that he can't appreciate me as I do him right now. How can you go from knowing everything to not knowing anything at all? Ugh, I hate his stupid depression. I guess I just need to surrender it all to God."

"*Filha,* depression is not an easy thing to deal with. And I know you love Declan more than any man you've ever loved before. But it is not fair that every day you wake up not knowing how he is going to act with you that day. His behavior has become so unpredictable, it's affecting you – to the point where I don't even know if I'm talking to my own daughter sometimes. Misery seeks company. And I don't want you to get depressed too.

"He disappeared once before. He may be a really good man, and he's always treated me with respect the couple of times I've met him over the years but I won't have it that he hurts you again. He has a lot of serious stuff going on."

I was surprised my father was even giving me any sort of reaction or opinion about Declan. Unlike other fathers I knew, he was always respectful of my love life, and never chimed in unless asked. But I also knew if he felt compelled to say something about the man I loved, it had to be for good reason. Either that, or he, too, had enough.

"I know, dad. You're absolutely right. It's just hard. I don't know what to do sometimes. He was so loving a couple of months ago and now – he doesn't even treat me like I'm his girlfriend."

"I've been there, my daughter. I went through it with your mom. Towards the last part of our marriage I always felt like I was walking on eggshells. I never knew when she would get mad out of nowhere. But you know what I've learned. There is only one person in this world I can trust."

"Who's that, dad?"

"God. You can always trust Him, my daughter. He will never leave you. He is always working behind the scenes to show you the way."

12:04 a.m. Journal Entry –

I did not think a month ago that depression would grip him so tightly as it has. I've been living in a world where every day contains an element of unpredictability. Declan and I have agreed that we will only see each other during Thanksgiving break, two months away. Bella has cheerleading events every weekend up until then that he needs to attend, so it only makes sense. He needs to focus on his stuff, he says, while not letting it affect me; and I need to focus on me. Yet, I'm drowning. I don't know what to think or what to believe. Who said depression and selfishness (because it is a damn bitch of nothing but selfishness) has to be a party of one? Our minds aren't immune to cracked realities, and our hearts aren't immune to pain. Mine is no exception.

I'm taken by this sadness, as it's starting to affect me, too. I want his kisses, his declaration of love, his sincerity and loving ways with me again. I want him to tell me how much he desires me and how much he craves to have me by his side. I want to wake up with his calls that make me smile. I want him to need me. I want him to tell me once more how much he wants to fuck the shit out of me and make sweet love to me. I want his soft side and compassionate nature back. I want this BS nonsense to go away and for time to be on our side. I know he is better than this, but he has left me vulnerable and confused.

September turned into October, and unlike the birds outside my apartment that moved so swiftly from one treetop to another, I was barely hanging on by a thread. Thanksgiving in November couldn't get here soon enough (isn't that the one time of year where everything goes back to being okay?).

Declan's depression was now in full swing, and hints of unresolved anger – that had nothing to do with me – started to creep though. He would snap at me over the smallest things. If I spent all day without hearing from him, Declan would scream and shout that he couldn't be bothered with explaining to me the hell he was going through. "You have no idea what I'm going through!" he would stammer, while I was left to wonder why he couldn't open up and share.

Soon I started to resent him for not asking about my day, and for making it seem like there weren't any solutions to any of his problems. You could offer a thousand answers, a thousand prayers, a thousand solutions – none were good enough in Declan's eyes.

I no longer knew when Declan was in pain, and I no longer had the tools to comfort him. In turn, it made me feel incredibly helpless, unloved and alone. How could I help a man who wouldn't let me in? How could I help a man who no longer cared if we went days without speaking? How could I help a man who no longer bothered to ask how I was doing? Soon I started to realize my father was right – I, too, was quickly succumbing to depression.

But I still wanted to hold onto hope with all my might. I knew how good things had been between us in the beginning, and I still believed our relationship could be salvaged, even if I saw it crumbling before me. Even if denial was at my doorstep.

For as long as I can remember, I've always been a fan of handwritten letters. Over the years I've collected boxes worth from friends, past lovers and family members alike. I knew letters were special to Declan, too. Since there was now no way of getting through to him in person or over the phone, I decided I would do the next best thing. For one-week straight, I would send him letters in the mail, every day. As a writer, composing handwritten letters came naturally to me, and it was something I truly took pleasure in. Whatever I was feeling or thinking that day, I would put to pen and paper and mail it off.

Toward the end of receiving my batch of letters, Declan called me one day before I started getting ready for bed. "I got all your letters," he said. "And I want you know I really appreciate them. I've always wanted a girl who would do that, and you do, so I'm very thankful. I just wish I wasn't in my current state with all these bullshit emotion-numbing situations. I know it's taking a toll on you."

A recent promotion at his job wasn't enough for him to feel the grips of depression loosen. The prospect of filing for bankruptcy due to the financial ruins his recent divorce put him in was still very much a potential reality. And Declan could feel the burden of paying a higher amount towards his daughter's private tuition, all while maintaining the mortgage on his five-bedroom home, which was a monstrosity he could have done without all together. There was nothing alleviating the dire financial situation he found himself in.

"I know I need to get rid of his house," he added. "I just know you would never think this was our house – and that's important to me. We'll have to start over, but hey, I'd rather you want the house we may eventually buy than live in one where you're never fully comfortable. I'm also fully aware that for you to move to Georgia, you will need more of a commitment from me.

These things don't go past me. Sometimes I don't open up because I don't want you to think I'm complaining all the time."

"Honey, I'm your partner, not your co-worker or an acquaintance. I want you to vent to me your frustrations. That's what I'm here for. Keeping it to yourself will only do damage."

"I love you," he said. "I know I should say it more often, but I just wanted you to know that I do."

And in that moment, that is all I needed to hear. So many days passed in a blur-like state that I had almost come to accept that he may have succumbed to his depression for good. But it was those moments when he still included me in his future decisions that I felt safe and secure for one more day. I needed him. I needed to continue to feel connected to him, and I knew he needed me, too. I just didn't know how long this feeling would last.

7:24 p.m. Journal Entry –

So. Needless to say, Declan's non-depressed state only lasted a good week. Meanwhile, his ever-changing mood swings are affecting me. Difference is, I have to suffer and deal with it alone. I feel like something's gotta give or I'm going to break. He's in an emotional shutdown mode again and not even trying to break free. Trying to talk to him is like talking to dry paint on the wall. I locked myself in my car today and screamed from the top of my lungs. Screaming out into the Universe! But nothing changes. Not only does nothing change but nothing gets better. Having to be this strong – for him, for us – is just downright, bloody cruel.

20

Despair

Days turned into weeks and weeks turned into months. The small glimpses of hope that everything was okay seemed to vanish just as soon as they materialized. Declan started to sink further and further into a deep state of depression, and his mood swings were draining me.

I had even turned to Google in a last attempt to be my psychologist and help me get some answers:

"What to do when your boyfriend is depressed"

"What to do during a manic episode"

"What's the difference between depression and bipolar"

"How do you recognize depression"

"How does alcohol affect depression"

But no matter how many times I read about first-hand accounts online of those who suffered from post-traumatic stress, and no matter how many times I pulled up articles on the *Psychology Today* website to see how I could more wisely and more effectively approach the situation, his demeanor with me was drastically taking a serious nosedive.

By this point, Declan and I were barely hanging on as lovers, and I was embarrassed to admit I had more conversations with my friends than I did with my own boyfriend. And we weren't just having your typical, run-of-the-mill arguments that most couples do from time to time. No, instead, simple inno-cent conversations would now often give way to full, blown-out fights. Fights that would leave me speechless and wondering, *how the fuck did this happen? Is he really getting this upset over nothing?*

Any kind of romance in our relationship was non-existent, too, as Declan had ceased flirting with me altogether. Gone were the days when he would surprise me with a racy text while I was at work, telling me how much he wished I was going down on him or fucking him hard. Gone were the days when he would call me to tell me he was getting off just thinking of me. Now, if I even approached the subject of fun and innocent sexual innuendos, he would fire back and let me know the thought of sex simply made him "sick." Needless to say, there was also no more space or room for any 'Deez Nutz' jokes for Deez Nutz were now left hanging in the wind. No pun intended.

Not too long before my scheduled Thanksgiving trip to Georgia, Declan and I were talking one night, just as I was leaving the gym. Even with all our visits to see each other, I still managed to find time to get my cardio in – and with his recent change of character, let's face it, it was also my way to stay sane.

On my way home from one of my typical workouts that consisted of too much weight lifting than what I would have usually liked, I called Declan to catch up with him about my day.

"I'm heading home now from the gym, but I'm so friggin tired. I only got five hours of sleep last night. Do you ever get tired, hun?" I asked, as I turned on the ignition to my car and threw my sweaty gym clothes in the back seat, not thinking anything about the comment I made or my innocent question.

I always knew Declan to be somebody to chime in with his opinions, but more and more, his comments were becoming aggressive and completely out of left field.

"Getting less than seven hours of sleep is detrimental to your health," he sternly pointed out. "You should not be doing that."

"Baaaabe, I understand. It's definitely not ideal but I've had a long day. So please. Instead of criticizing, I would just appreciate it if you're supportive, okay?"

"No, Maíra. I will not fucking support this bad behavior!" he remarked. "This is a red flag to me!"

Bad behavior? Sure, five hours of sleep wasn't ideal but it certainly wasn't bad behavior. I was in shock. And the more we spoke, the more frustrated I got. Although oftentimes in the past, I would bite my tongue in an attempt to diffuse the situation and calm Declan down, I was tired. Really *damn tired* of the crazy ups and downs and enormous level of unpredictability I had to deal with what seemed like every single day now. No matter which way you looked at it, I couldn't win when it came to us. There was suddenly always something Declan found to berate me about.

I was tired that the entire divorce fiasco – even though it was finally over and done with – still had a strong hold on him, because he now had a tainted view on love. I was tired that if Declan didn't have enough money in the bank account, or his car broke down, that he was then given a free card to treat me like well, *shit.* I was tired that every time I tried to be affectionate and loving toward him, he turned me away. I was tired that I was forced to be celibate for a full year, not by choice, but in support and respect for a man that I loved. I was tired of us arguing over the dumbest things such as how many hours of sleep I got last night, or if Hillary Clinton was in the wrong for not speaking to her supporters the night she lost the Presidential Election.

I was tired of making so many sacrifices to see him again and again, to fly to Georgia then immediately drive down to Melbourne so he would never have to be alone – *and for what.* I was tired that sometimes I would go all day long without hearing from him as if it was normal. I was tired of giving him my heart and being vulnerable just as he asked me to, and getting nothing in return. And even though I understood that some things he simply couldn't control, and it was the disgusting nature of this depression game, I did not know how much longer I could keep my head above water.

"You know what!" I stormed. "I've tried really fucking hard to be more patient than fucking Dalai Lama as well as mature about a number of things with you, Declan! But I will not let you harp on five hours like it's the end of the world. Because the big picture is far more serious and it has nothing to fucking do with me!" Through unexpected waves of heated passion, just bursting from my lips, my anger got the best of me.

For three days Declan and I did not speak. I gathered we just needed some time to collect our thoughts. And even though it was a heat-of-the-moment thing for the both of us, it was nothing we couldn't work through. I figured we would come together after both of us calmed down and we would continue to walk through these murky waters together.

So I went about my business, engrossing myself with all my managing editorial responsibilities at work and calling up one of my friends when I needed to vent. Eventually, he would get out of his depression again, I thought, and we would find ourselves in a better place, just as it was back in August. But while my mind was telling me one thing, my heart was telling me another. I could feel that something terrible was about to happen.

"Honey, I don't want to fight. Please just listen to me," I said, texting him a few days later when I realized Declan still refused to budge and break the ice. It was another hot and muggy afternoon in Broward, even as we approached the turkey-baking joys of Thanksgiving. I had spent a good portion of my day doing my nails at a salon just down the street, right by the Starbucks I frequently visited. Anything to distract me from the tumbling pieces of my relationship that I was struggling to keep from falling.

I often painted my nails a color that reflected my mood and today was no exception. "Give me the blackest black you have," I told the nail lady. And as I waited for Declan to write me back, I asked her to add another coat.

Hours passed before Declan finally responded. The text was so long, it took a couple of scroll-downs to see it in its entirety. *This couldn't be good.*

"Maíra, I've come to realize that I'm really, really damaged, both emotionally and mentally. There's nothing you can do and only time will help me.

I feel the coldness inside of me, and the need to control situations so I don't show vulnerability. You deserve the best of me, and I haven't even been able to give you a sliver of that. I love you but I lack the capacity to show it. It's obvious I can't be in a relationship right now. And while you say you want to walk the fire with me, I can't allow that. It's killing me to see how my behavior is affecting you. I'm so sorry."

I was in tears. I ushered the nail lady to finish my manicure and hurry up and soon I was walking back home with black nail polish smudged all over one of my favorite gym shirts.

No, this can't be over. We can't just give up when the going gets rough. We can't let his depression win. We can work this out. I know we can. Right?

"Declan…. I may be devastated but I'm going to see you as we planned," I wrote back, my hands shaking, still unable to grasp his gut-wrenching words. "Remember, love is patient. Love is kind. Love keeps no record of wrongdoings. I know you have so much you feel you have to overcome but I won't let you make me be that person that made you 'better' for someone else. My love for you is genuine. You know that, right?"

"You can still come up here. I'm not going to leave you hanging at the airport. I might be an asshole but I'm not a dick," he said, without even taking a second to acknowledge my love for him, and while I wondered if being an *asshole* or a *dick* weren't one and the same.

My Thanksgiving trip to Georgia was now only mere days away. After two long months of counting down the days until I would be in his arms again, I could have never predicted I'd fly to see Declan again under these very different terms. *A stupid breakup.* A breakup I simply couldn't accept. The deepest parts of me were crying out, trying to make sense of anything that lay before me. I was angry. I was pissed. But I was also ready to put on my superwoman gear and venture into fighting mode. Whatever it took, I was ready.

I was not willing to let go of him or this love that easily. We had come too damn far.

21

Thanksgiving Trip

Rather than excited and energized, for the first time I was flying to Georgia in a state of despair. While friends and co-workers alike looked forward to upcoming Thanksgiving festivities – whether it was taking a relaxing cruise to the Bahamas or layering up for the chilly air at NYC's Macy's parade – I braced myself for whatever was to come with Declan. We were left hanging by a thread, and I tried with all my might to hang on to dear life.

"You deplane yet?"

Declan was already at the airport waiting for me, as I thought about whether I should simply not walk down the runway and turn around and go home. Delta Airlines had became my close companion in recent months, and I didn't want to leave the safe confines of the plane – the only thing I had left in what was now becoming a *shit storm*. I almost hoped the flight attendant would hold my hand as I braved Georgia one more time.

"Yes, on train." I texted back.

"Okay. The airport arrival is a fucking disaster. Hang out by baggage claim. I'm coming in. Actually, come to Delta check-in. I'm between baggage claim 1 and 2."

I didn't want to see him. I was too nervous to see him. *Maybe I wasn't so ready after all.* Then leaning against a wall on the right side of the Delta baggage claim carousel, he was there. He looked around, still trying to find me amongst dozens of strangers in this obscure late-night airport crowd. Declan's now-long brown hair was gelled back, and a tight-fitted pair of jeans accentuated his butt. He was wearing a denim long-sleeved shirt I never saw before; one I thought he picked up recently after insisting he needed new clothes.

On the other hand, nothing I wore indicated I was there to dress to impress, because I wasn't. All I wanted was to see how I could *possibly talk Declan out of thinking we reached a dead end. Maybe we could go on a break.* Maybe we just needed to talk things out. Anything but this.

I tapped Declan on the shoulder as I placed my luggage next to him on the polka-dotted, tacky floor. He turned around smiling and gave me a big hug. "Hey, hey. How was the trip?"

I was straining to show any kind of enthusiasm, any hint that I was happy to see him despite everything, but Declan could see right through me. This trip would be different from all the others. I knew it, and he knew it; and neither of us knew what to do about it.

Heading back to his place during that all-too-familiar drive outside Atlanta, I could tell Declan was trying to find the right words to get many things off his chest.

"I want you to know, Maíra, that I've started taking some anti-depressant herbal medication, and they seem to be working," he said, steering down the highway.

"Oh yeah? When did you start taking them?"

"Yesterday. I'm feeling better now. And I know all of your friends probably think I'm an asshole and are just as bewildered that you would even come up here after everything that's happened."

"They don't think you're an asshole, Declan. Far from it. They understand you're depressed, and they try to help me better understand that. Because you know it's a struggle for me, too. And if we are to truly break up, I want us to have a talk first. A good, heart-to-heart talk."

"Okay, go ahead."

"No, not here. Not right now. We're just driving to your place for crying out loud, and I know you'll go to bed as soon we arrive." I managed to let out a chuckle. How could I forget how much Declan loved to sleep early.

"No, no. We can stay up and talk. We need to," he said, as we pulled off the Barrett Knoll Parkway exit to his house. I also want you to know something else, and you have to promise you will never use this against me, okay? So, you know how you said in that text of yours that you were going to fight for me, that you weren't going to let me be a better man for someone else?"

"Mhmm."

"Well, that's exactly the kind of woman I need. It meant a lot when you said that."

The light poles on the streets of Kennesaw flickered as we drove past them. The roads were quiet and still. Unlike in South Florida, I couldn't remember a time I ever saw people hustling about late at night here in Georgia. It was almost 11 p.m. by the time we pulled up to Declan's driveway. Ozzy was already barking, wondering who his dad could possibly be bringing home. "Hey buddy! I missed you!" I said, as he jumped up on me, almost knocking my purse from in between my arm when I walked inside.

"Do you wanna take your stuff upstairs?" asked Declan.

"Nah, I'm okay for now. We can do that later. I think I just need a moment to relax. Not gonna lie, feels weird being here again. Seeing you and stuff. I waited so long to come here again and I missed you so much and then – oh, nevermind."

"I know, Maíra. I know. It's all a mess. Anyway. What are some of the things you wanted to talk to me about? We can talk about them now if you want. I'm not even tired."

He had laid down on an adjoining loveseat beside me now and taken off his shoes. All the rooms in his five-bedroom house looked clean and spotless, even as I observed them from downstairs. *He must have tidied everything up for me.* I wondered how much I should speak from the heart, or if I should just let him do all the talking.

"I don't even know where to begin," I sighed. "Like I said, I'm not going down without a fight. I love you. I've *always* loved you. And if you need time, you can take all the time you need – but I don't want to lose you. How did we even get to this point? I hate that your depression is getting the best of you. I really *fucking* do."

He rubbed his eyes as if to let out a deep sigh then sat up straight. Ozzy was already knocked out, dozing away by his half-empty water bowl, and leaving us to figure out whatever unanswered questions we had between us on our own.

"I don't know how this all happened either," said Declan. I'm still trau-matized by everything that happened this year. From my brother passing to the stupid marriage to the money stuff to I can't even bring myself to be intimate with you – I feel like I can't seem to catch a break. But it's more than that. I feel like I no longer look at love with innocent eyes."

"How so?" I asked. I wasn't sure if I should look at him directly now, or continue to hide my tears I felt creeping up my throat.

"Let me explain," he began. "There have only been two women in my life that I felt were 'keepers.' One was this girl I dated in college years ago – she was just like you, very loving and giving – and the other person is you. And yet I still fuck it up. There's this saddened wisdom that's come over me, and I just don't know how to find my way back from it."

"But I don't understand, Declan. You know I would never hurt you. Why can't you just open up to me again? Why have you allowed yourself to become so callous and cold?" At this point I had already shifted my sitting position toward him. I wanted to make sure I didn't miss a single look, a single sigh – his body language was completely on my radar.

"I'm not sure, Maíra. It's my way of protecting myself," he said, making eye contact with me only to then look away and focus his eyes on the car-peted, vacuumed floor. "I simply don't want to allow myself to be vulnerable.

Not after everything I went through this year. I don't want to let anyone in and I don't want to care about anybody else's feelings but my own. It's fucked up, I know. But it's where I am right now. And there's something else… but you can't get mad at me. Promise me you won't."

"I can't promise I won't get mad, but I can promise I'll still be here," I said, as he now struggled to maintain any kind of eye contact.

" Okay… so. Umm. How do I say this. So the other day – I had suicidal thoughts again and I almost bought a kit online to just pull the plug."

"Oh, Declan. Honey. I'm so sorry." I wanted to reach out my hand and touch him but I knew there was no other better time than now to give him his space. For a moment, I could feel another presence in the living room. Another presence just trying to guide me in my love for him, even if I was at the verge of losing the one man I absolutely loved. So as I had done months ago, I took the opportunity to simply reach out as a friend.

"I don't want you to feel that way, babe. As much as I know you, I can never tell when you're really at a deep end. I'm here for you."

"I ended up not buying the kit, I'll have you know. You know, just in case you're wondering and all. Again, I had another moment where something just talked me out of it. Please don't be mad." I could sense a sigh of relief that he was telling me this. The hairs on his arms were no longer raised, and the veins in his neck had softened.

"I'm not. I just hurt for you. Blah. I hate this. I seriously hate this. Can I ask you something?"

"Sure."

"What did the other girls you previously dated do when you were depressed?"

"Well, to be honest with you, they didn't really know I was depressed. I don't think I was ever with them long enough for them to know," he laughed. "Only Bella's mom knew towards the second half of our marriage, but she didn't care. She thought I had to suck it up and get it together. She didn't truly see it as a mental illness. You're the only one since who's really seen so much of it. "

"I'm so sorry. I wish there was more I could do."

"Unfortunately, there's nothing you can do. Only God can help me out of this."

I didn't know how we could step away from our emotionally-drawn heavy conversations. Only an hour after landing in Georgia, I was already wishing I could hop on the first flight back home. For the first time ever, I didn't feel comfortable here. By the looks of it, there was no saving me, and there was no saving Declan either.

Somehow or another, though, at some point during the night Declan and I switched gears to more lighthearted, intriguing topics that were random as they were morbidly fascinating. From sex robots of the future to theories of the afterlife, you would have never known we had been talking about the complexities of our own relationship just an hour before. By the time we got ready to head upstairs and climb into bed, it was already past 2 a.m. Our future was now unclear, and it seemed like that was how it would remain.

I got up the next morning to the cool silence of Thanksgiving Day and Declan still quietly asleep with Ozzy between us in bed. Later in the afternoon a dinner reservation awaited us at Aspens Steakhouse, the same location I previously sampled my favorite mac and cheese.

I thought about how the day would transpire. For the first time I saw our relationship in a state of limbo, and I didn't know which course of action to take. There was no telling which direction anything was bound to go.

Closer to noon, Declan got out of bed and I followed him downstairs for a cup of coffee. I reminded him about our dinner reservations, and we agreed we would call an hour ahead of time to confirm. His demeanor was solemn and so was mine. I blamed it on us talking each other's ear off the night before.

"Did you see the new coffee machine I have in the kitchen?" he asked, pointing to his fancy-schmansy Keurig coffee machine, the latest talk in all of caffeinated town.

"Oh yeah. I was wondering if I had seen it before."

"My dad brought it when he came to visit."

"What do you mean 'your dad brought it here when he came to visit'? When was your dad even here?"

"Umm. A couple of weeks ago or maybe even before that. I don't remember."

"Wait. Your dad was here visiting and you forgot to casually mention it in any of our conversations?"

Although the night before we seemed to have been able to squash any tension between us, I was now starting to get upset. I couldn't believe that Declan had become so detached from me that he couldn't even remember to fill me in on his day-to-day life anymore. Especially when I knew his father had never seen his new place in Georgia before.

"Yes, Maíra, my dad was here. Guess I forgot to tell you or something."

"Ugh, Declan. I just can't. It's a big deal that your father finally came to see your place in Georgia for the first time. I can't believe you didn't think of sharing this with me. Like, really?"

Not wanting to create an even bigger scene, I grabbed my cup of coffee and marched back up the stairs. I could hear Declan yelling behind me. "You see, Maíra, this is why I can't be in a relationship!"

I shut the door behind me as I stormed into Declan's room and threw myself on his bed. I pulled the silk covers over me and cried into his pillow, hoping it would muffle any sounds from reaching downstairs. I knew we were done. It had not even been a full day since I landed and we were already fighting again. I knew there was no way I could stay here for the next four days, and though a part of me didn't want to go home just yet, I knew it would probably be for the best. Not just for me, but for the both of us.

After Declan insisted nothing good could be gained if I stayed, I rebooked my flight to fly back home in 24 hours. Just like that, we were back to square one. In the meantime, Declan and I went about our business, not saying a word to each other. While I remained upstairs for a good part of the day, he stayed downstairs catching up on any kind of Netflix binge-worthy show. It was impossible to even try or consider having fun together. Yup, our stupid fight had now officially ruined the entire trip, as well as the meaning of Thanksgiving. And our reservation at Aspens came and went with neither one of us calling to confirm or cancel.

Eventually the rumblings of my stomach led me back downstairs in search of something to eat. There was so much I wanted to say to Declan, and I begged and prayed for God to just get rid of this awkward tension between us.

"Declan, I still can't understand. You say you can't be in a relationship – okay, fine! But ugh. Did it really have to come to this?" I said, trying to hold back my tears, while Declan seemed to remain calm and unaffected by anything I had to say. "Ugh. I swear, sometimes I feel like I just hate you!"

At that moment he hit pause on the remote control than sat up on the couch to face me. His Netflix show could wait. Ozzy, wanting no part of a match of shouting words, scurried his way to the back patio.

"You just don't get it, do you?" By now his tone had turned stern yet sincere. "So go on, Maíra. Say everything you want to say. Let me have it! But for crying out loud, just understand this. I am doing this to protect you – the one woman I love, okay?! And there's more. Don't you get it? I don't want to fucking hurt you, and it kills me to see you this way. That's what it fucking comes down to but we can't be in this relationship. We both acted on impulse, period."

"Tell me why you love me, Declan!" I shouted. "Tell me right here! Right now! Tell me fucking why!" With my hands on my hips, I stood before him with a dead-set look in my eyes, hoping for any sign that he would show me that, beneath it all, he still remembered what it was like to love me. I needed an answer. A clear and straight answer for once.

"I don't know, Maíra. I just don't know anything right now! And I'm so fucking sorry!"

"You can't even give me a goddamn reason why you love me! What in the world?! Are you serious? What am I doing here, God? This is fucking torture!"

I was in no state of mind or place of heart to hear anything more. All that needed to be said was said, and every single word cut right through me, only intensifying the pain. In a matter of hours, I would fly home trying to barely hold onto any sliver of dignity I had left. I hated how Declan's depression had completely changed him. And yet what he failed to see was that, even though he could no longer register his feelings for me, I, on the other hand, had never been more sure of my love for him.

I couldn't sleep that night, and while Declan decided to sleep on the couch, I retreated to his bedroom one last time. When the sun rose, I didn't waste a second to pack my bags while Declan took Ozzy on his usual morning walk around the neighborhood. I was crawling in my skin and anxious to leave. If Declan didn't want me here, there was no reason for me to stay.

While I waited for them to return, I noticed a two-page letter with my name on it, in Declan's handwriting, sitting by my purse that I had left the night before at the front door. That's funny, I thought. How didn't I see this before? I pulled up one of the kitchen chairs to where I stood. Not knowing what contents I would find on these pages, I wanted to make sure I was sitting down for this. And so I began reading.

Maíra, I haven't written a letter to anyone in a long time so pardon me if I end up rambling. You are the kindest, most loving, big hearted, emphathetic, thoughtful, selfless person I have ever met. Even in this awful situation, you have maintained a level of maturity that is impressive. I deserve you. You have expressed the exact type of person and qualities I want. You, though, deserve better.

Unfortunately, my behavior is lessening you. I can't and won't let my broken-ness and toxicity change you more than what I fear it already has. I am walking away because your compassion, love and commitment won't let you when it's clear you should.

Love, Declan.

I sat there, motionless, enveloped by my tears and clutching my legs like a baby. Although a stack of letters that I had mailed Declan over the past few months remained in his office, this was the first time he had ever written me a note of his own. Suddenly the realization hit me: I didn't know how I would possibly begin to move on from this breakup. I didn't know how I would possibly find the air to breathe without him. Nothing felt more impossible. But at least I had this letter, the one thing from him I would forever cherish and hold as sacred.

The ride to the airport was short yet grueling. So many questions were still running inside my head, but by now I realized there was no point in entertaining the idea of getting any concrete answers. Declan and I were going around in circles and one of us had to press on the brakes and bring it to a complete stop. But I still had just one more thing I needed to know.

"Declan, what's gonna happen with us from here on out?" I asked as I noticed we had less than 10 minutes to go before he pulled up to the Atlanta airport.

"I have no idea…." he said, not flinching to briefly look at me.

I sighed, knowing it wasn't exactly the answer I wanted to hear. I couldn't read Declan anymore. I had felt like I knew his heart for months – but now – we drove to the airport in almost complete silence, as if annoyed at the fact that we had to sit next to each other before I made it to my flight.

"Can you at least promise that you will reach out to me when you need me. Promise me that even if you feel it would be a burden on me you'll still reach out. Promise?" I hoped against all hope that he would give me something to hold onto.

"I promise."

I already knew the Delta Airlines sign at the Departures section of the airport like the back of my hand. Though Declan and I said goodbye many times before, this time I wondered if it would be for good. I wanted to hug him and never let go as I did so many times before. Instead, I helped him pick up my stuff and place it on a luggage cart after he parked his car on the sidewalk.

"You've got everything you need, right?" he asked. I didn't know if he was looking straight at me or just rushing to give me my carry-on so I could leave.

I nodded.

I hesitated to look at him, afraid I'd stare into those dark eyes I had fallen in love with one last time and see them not look back at me with the same tender love and care. I wanted to just feel him lean in and cradle me in his arms and kiss me and make love to me like he did two years ago and just forget that any of this ever happened. Forget that any of this ever had to happen.

"Text me when you get home, okay? Let me know you got home safe," he said.

I wanted to tell Declan that I loved him, that I still love him and that I will forever love him. *No matter what.* I wanted to scream and shout my love for him like the first day we met when I knew, here, there was something special. *But what for, he already knows.*

I reassured him I would get in touch after I landed then I grabbed my things and walked through those all-too-familiar Delta gates one more time. With my eyes forward, I disappeared behind a couple of glass-screened doors, obscuring the outside world and hoping I would never have to face it again. Straight out of a movie, I was now that sad girl, empty and alone, with my heart in my throat and a future that was now just a memory of what-could-have-been.

Not in the mood to exchange pleasantries with strangers, I sat down by a trash bin a few feet away from my gate, just waiting for the flight announcer to start calling passengers on board. I didn't care that I sat on a germ-infested floor that had God knows what on it. Nothing mattered anymore. Not what I wanted. Not how I felt. And surely not how I looked. Slowly, one by one, they started to allow passengers to board. I waited patiently until I was the last one in line.

My window seat was toward the back of the plane, in a row I had all to myself. I debated whether or not to write in my journal, just to kill the time and get all the *muck* out on paper. But then, against my better judgment, I decided I didn't want to write about how much *shit really hit the fan*. I gazed out to the sky and hopelessly begged any kind of divine force to intervene. Anything to save me from this pain. But who was I kidding. Only dark clouds could hear me, and nobody could see me. Not my best friend. Not my dad. Not even God himself.

22

The Dream

"**N**othing's gonna hurt you, baby. As long as you're with me, you'll be just fine."

I can hear those lyrics and melodies swirling around in my head. The dream feels so real and vivid still. I can still see the dream remarkably sharp and clear, just like that time it awoke me a week after Declan and I broke up and had me rushing to call my best friend the following day in tears. Only wishing it had been real.

I see us like I've never seen us before. My mind instantly captures the lyrics of that all-familiar song by Cigarettes After Sex I dedicated to Declan once, as I had the tendency to do with almost every song I heard, time and time again.

We've been here before, or rather, I've been here before. I know where every picture frame stands in Declan's living room. His house keys continue to dangle on top of the kitchen counter, and his protein powder container sits by the sink. Except for the times I flipped through certain passages of Scripture, the Holy Bible that was given to him by his friend has pages unturned. His dog is happy to greet us with his front paws over our laps, as he does every time, asking us to acknowledge and play with him.

I didn't think I would be back here again. It had been so long. So many memories that cling onto this house, of magical times when we declared and prayed over our love for each other, and other days where the tears on my suitcase was the only thing that provided me solace going home.

This time it's different. I waited and hoped to see him again. One more time. But I knew better than to expect anything else of it. Until now. Gazing over at him from my usual spot on the sofa, I watch as he makes his way to the wine cooler to pick out some sophisticated Merlot, one that is just for special occasions, special invitations or special guests. There has only been one other time in all these months that he has popped open an expensive wine just for us.

He pours and we drink and he pours and we drink some more. That smile I have always loved about him makes its way toward me again. I am drunk off fleeting nostalgia and a sweet desire that seems like it is all mine to hold.

"Come upstairs with me," he whispers, as he grabs my hand and leads me down the hallway to his bedroom, stopping short as we get to the door. He is looking at me intently. It is a look I have maybe only seen once before that speaks of regret for not having done this sooner, and a determination to finally see it through. To see through these beating hearts and a stupid zipper that simply needs to come undone.

Here before us is an aching passion that cannot not be contained anymore.

With my hands up, he lifts my loose shirt, removes my bra and tosses them behind him. Before I can even make my way inside his room, I can feel the warmth of his body over mine. Unable to utter a word, he kisses me without warning, trapping me in a state of submission.

"I want to make love to you... I don't want to wait any longer," he implores.

The more he kisses me, the more delirious I feel. I am at the mercy of his touch, of his words, and of promises that I am the only one who matters. The only one who *ever* mattered.

Our clothes lay in a perfect heap on the floor, with nothing but the faint light in the hallway to illuminate the deep longing we have wrestled with for far too long. The lines on his face tell the story of a man who is ready to let go, to let vulnerability take its comfortable retreat on his lap. For I am here. I have always been here, and I'm not willing to walk away.

I crave him in a way a woman should never crave a man. Like he is my breath of life, and I cannot make sense of my own being if he is not part of it. My every truth, my every pain and my every longing belongs to him. He is the only one I have *ever* needed.

The cold sheets beneath me caress my back, as the soft outline of his body draws me in closer. He is on top of me now, and the perfect alignment of our bodies gives him permission to enter. I want him to make his presence known, to act on this hunger that he cannot continue to ignore. I do not know how to patiently wait anymore. It has been too many months of surrendering to a love that has completely raptured me, yet denied me the tender affection and ravishing passion I so deserve.

I can feel a single tear slowly make its way down the corner of my eye and wash away everything that was thought to be in vain. *I've waited for this for so long...*

I can feel the light fade around me then spin in circles until we both let go. I do not have to pretend anymore. I want him to fuck me and make love to me and give me every damn piece of him. With each beckoning move and tantalizing thrust, I want him even more. There is no turning back. Every time he lets the world around him collapse inside of me, he is also one step closer to finding himself again.

And so am I.

23

Horizon

After a breakup, time seems to come to a complete standstill. The minutes drag on, the days never end and you suddenly have no idea what to do with yourself anymore. Plus, the fact that you are awoken by far too often vivid, wet dreams doesn't help.

Not soon after I arrived back home in Florida the day after Thanksgiving, my pillowcases quickly became my daily punching bags and a number of blank notebooks became the therapy I couldn't afford. I was in a state of shock, and I did not know how I would pick up the pieces and move on without Declan, so I did the only thing I knew how: I made the conscious decision that, at the turn of the New Year, I would no longer put my dreams on hold. If there was any way I would be able to bear this heartache, I had to start making my life about me and distract myself from any and all thoughts of him. So I began writing this memoir, and I began to follow through on what God said to me on the Pacific Crest Trail in Oregon. I realized it was time I actively seek employment in Georgia.

I confided in only a couple of my closest friends about my search. I created a work profile online, updated my resume and sent out applications almost daily. I knew I wanted to continue my professional career in the editorial field, so when I found an editorial position for the leading online source of health information, and it seemed to match my skillset and professional background to a tee, I applied immediately. A day later, I got an email response: "We see you are in Florida. We just wanted to inform you that this position is located in Atlanta, Georgia."

"Yes, I understand," I wrote back. "I am looking to relocate to Georgia, given the right opportunity."

A few days later, I was completing a phone interview, and a week after that, I was flying up to Atlanta for an in-person meeting with four employees of one of the biggest companies in the nation. Everything was suddenly happening so fast, I almost didn't have time to dwell on my current state of miserable affairs.

Days, followed by weeks, slowly began to pass and I no longer felt suffocated by my pain. I was so immersed in my job search and determination to leave Florida that I had no time to succumb to my heartache. Every now and again, I heard from Declan, but it wasn't the same. If he was still depressed, I could no longer tell, because he was now completely distant, reserved and detached. A transparent carbon copy of a person I didn't recognize anymore. While I was dealing with the pain and suffering of our breakup, he still chose to not address any matters regarding us. As far as he was concerned, the traumatic events that happened to him were still reason enough to push me away, to push everyone away – even the woman he loved.

After I was asked to fly up to Atlanta for an in-person job interview, I contemplated whether or not to tell Declan that I would be in town. I wondered if it could do any good to see him again. I ultimately decided I'd give him the heads up about my trip, but I would leave the ball in his court about seeing me. If he approached the subject of meeting up, I would welcome it.

"I have my daughter this weekend, but I can see about leaving her with her mom early so we can meet up," he texted me the day I landed. "Then you can get back to your AirBnB place to catch up on some sleep before the interview. "Cool?"

The weekend before my job interview in Atlanta, I booked an AirBnB just 10 minutes away from Midtown, in a run-down, sketchy part of Downtown that had me second-guessing whether I still wanted to move to Georgia.

Declan and I agreed that he would pick me up at 6 p.m. that Sunday evening for a quick dinner at a casual café nearby. "I know just the spot you'd like," he said.

I thought about what I would say as I got dressed to meet him. So many things had been left unsaid. Maybe this was my opportunity to tell him how much pain I was still in. Maybe this was my opportunity to tell him how much I was still madly in love with him, even if I couldn't understand or explain it myself. Maybe, just maybe, he would come to his senses and tell me what a fool he was to end our relationship so prematurely. Or maybe, this time, I was hoping for a dream that would simply never come to be again.

With my new floral jacket on and a double coat of super black mascara to make my eyes pop, I stepped outside the AirBnB apartment to see Declan's car parked on the corner of a side street, not in exactly the safest parts of town. My hands started to tremble, and my breath got heavier the closer I got to the passenger door. I wasn't sure I was ready to see him again for the first time in three months. *Calm yourself, Maíra,* I tried reminding myself. *It's okay. You'll get through this. Just act nonchalant."*

Declan was fixated on the steering wheel when I tapped on the car window and climbed inside his BMW. "Hey, how's it going?" I muttered as I tried to avoid eye contact, knowing full well it would only make me melt inside if those eyes I fell in love with interlocked with mine.

No nice-to-see-you-agains were exchanged. Not like before when Declan often greeted me with a compliment upon seeing me. The air between was cold and dry, as if it had been sliced through with a knife hours before we met. His dark hair was neatly combed back, and his frame was smaller, thus enhancing his broad shoulders and his muscular arms.

I gathered he had lost a bit of weight, and I hated him for looking better than the last time I saw him. I could tell he was really putting in the work for a summer fitness competition he told me about when we were still together. And here I was, looking like my head and body had gotten spun in a blender then tossed out to dry on a clothing hanging line. I was still a mess.

From the second I saw Declan, it was clear I was overly dressed for the occasion. While I made sure to straighten my hair and meticulously take my time doing my makeup, Declan looked like he picked out whatever pair of jeans and shoes he found lying around his house. He was certainly not trying to impress me. Not this time. Yup, times had definitely changed.

In the middle of I-don't-know-where, Declan and I pulled up to a small eatery joint that was far too casual for my liking. Again, I was more overly dressed than I would have liked to admit, but I knew I had to go with it. The last thing I wanted was to feel any friction with us the night before my big interview.

After our waitress directed us to a window booth with the glow of a faint candle on our table, I looked out into the parking lot, trying hard to keep my brewing emotions at bay. I was tense and still resentful. The past suddenly lurched back at me and grabbed me by the throat. Although, typically, I would have been so happy to see Declan, this time I couldn't even force a fake smile on my face even if I tried. I was still in pain, and to make it worse, I wasn't anywhere close to being over him.

In order to avoid the undeniable awkwardness of seeing each other for the first time post-breakup, we began to update each other on current happenings in our lives. My best friend Oceana recently became pregnant, I shared.

"It was unexpected," I said, "But she is doing the best she can given the circumstances."

"Oh, wow," he gasped, suddenly wide-eyed. "That sucks. Man, that sure makes me glad I did that vasectomy. I would hate to deal with an unexpected pregnancy. Sorry to hear that."

Barely able to dig in to the chicken dinner entrees that had already made its way to us, I listened to Declan as he continued to spew shards of insensitive words and remarks I could have done without. And then as the topic switched to his job, and how he couldn't even talk to the women there because he didn't trust anyone, I found myself getting nauseous. I couldn't believe how careless he could be saying these things in front of me, to the woman he insisted on building a future with just a few months ago.

I could feel traces of my super-black mascara coming undone, and the color in my face draining and leaving my body, hoping against all hope that it could just leave this world.

"Is everything okay?" asked Declan, for a moment appearing almost concerned. Not one to fool him, I knew I couldn't lie to him. He could always tell when I wasn't being myself.

"I think I'm going to be sick," I said under my breath. "I'm sorry, just give me a moment. I need to go to the bathroom."

Grabbing my small purse, I quickly made a dash to the nearest toilet stall in the women's bathroom. The walls around me were cold, and for a moment, I thought I was shivering and dissolving into a crumpled up ball at the mercy of my own haywire emotions. I was alone. Alone in this moment, and alone in my continued adoration and love for him.

I took in a few deep breaths and then let myself have a good cry once I realized nobody was in the bathroom with me. There was no getting through to Declan. I could see now that I was holding onto something that was only in my head. There was nothing left to hold onto.

After I gently wiped away my streaked mascara with mounds of toilet paper, I returned to the window booth where Declan was waiting for me, confused.

"Are you going to tell me what's going on?"

I let out a deep sigh. "Okay, only because I've always been transparent with you. Declan, I'm sitting here in front of you after not seeing you for months since our breakup, and you're killing me with some of the things you've said. I know you're not trying to intentionally cause me pain, but goddamn. You say some things that I don't even think you realize how hurtful they can actually be.

217

"For starters, you're telling me how relieved you feel that you got a vasectomy when just six months ago, we were trying to book an appointment for a reversal so we could start planning to have our own family for crying out loud."

"Maíra," he interrupted. "Who I was six months ago is not who I am today. I know I'm being a dick but right now it's working for me. I'm all about me right now."

I was taken back by his words. No emotion. No remorse. Nothing to indicate he still gave a damn. I could no longer deny that his brother's passing, his poisonous second marriage – and what I deemed to be elements of post-traumatic stress – still profoundly affected his behavior toward me. Or maybe he was just using everything as an excuse to be a narcissistic, no-good person I didn't want to be around. I wondered for how much longer he would continue to use everything that happened to him as an excuse to treat me so poorly.

"Wow, Declan. Okay. You know what. That's all you need to say to me."

What was supposed to be a nice evening filled with smiles and laughter and stomach butterflies became nothing short of an uncomfortable and awkward disaster. I immediately shut down, recoiled into my own skin and wished I could suddenly hate him with every ounce of my being. I was ready to go home, ready to once again, as it was months before, turn to my pillow to console me through my tears.

I struggled to fall asleep that night, my job interview was only a few hours away, and it required me to paint on a smile, put on my big-girl pants and pretend everything was okay. I needed to make a good impression yet inside I felt anything but excited and optimistic.

That Monday, after a two-hour meeting with several company managers and supervisors in Midtown Atlanta, I hopped on the first evening flight back to Fort Lauderdale. "We'll make our decision within a week or so," said Paige, a darling woman close to my age, who relocated to Georgia from Tennessee and was hiring for the position.

Settled back in South Florida, I scheduled a full day's worth of self-pampering at the local spa for the following day, which also happened to be my birthday and a much-needed day off from work. Determined to forget about everything and everyone, I spent a few hours basking in the soft sounds of aromatherapy music, while blackheads were eradicated from the surface of my skin and my butt was exposed to a ceiling of dim lighting as I got a complete hands-on body massage.

As I was getting ready to head home mid-afternoon with my face aglow and my back cracked in all the right places, my cell phone rang. It was an Atlanta area code. Strange, I thought, I was told they would make their decision in a week. Maybe something came up.

"Hello?" I answered.

"Hi Maíra. This is the recruiter calling from your job interview yesterday. How are you? Can I get five minutes of your time?"

"Oh, hey! I'm doing well, thank you. Yes, of course. I'm not working today since it's my birthday so I can definitely talk. How may I help you?"

"It's your birthday? How nice! Well, hopefully I have some good birthday news to share with you. We would like to offer you the position here in Atlanta if you are interested."

"What?! Oh my god. Really? That is incredible! Yes, I'm most certainly interested! Thank you so much! You just made my birthday," I beamed.

"I'm glad I could help," the recruiter laughed. "These are some of the perks of my job, sharing some good news. There is only one thing: We need you to start in exactly a month."

Without knowing anything or anyone in Atlanta (I was familiar with suburbia Kennesaw, but not the capital of the state), I knew time was not on my side. I had four weeks to figure out where to live, how I was going to move my belongings and what would be the name of the new neighborhood I would call home.

Oceana was now three months pregnant, and since I was concerned that the freezing Georgia winter would make my dad's health take a turn for the worse, I realized I had to figure out many of these moving matters on my own. Thankfully, within a day, a co-worker immediately put me in touch with a realtor they knew in the Peach State, and the following weekend I found myself flying back up to Georgia to secure an apartment in place. My dream to leave Florida was finally coming true, though in much different circumstances than what I ever expected.

Founded in 2012 as its own established, Brookhaven is a cozy, affluent neighborhood right outside Atlanta. As much as I loved Kennesaw, it was too far from my workplace (and it probably wouldn't have been a good idea to stay too geographically close to Declan anyway), so I decided I had to look for something that felt like the suburbs, yet gave me close-enough access to everything I needed.

Recommended by my realtor, Brookhaven was the right setting for young professionals and small families, only a 20-minute drive from my new job. Surrounded by color-changing leaves and sky-high trees, I knew I could feel at ease here during my first year. Six days after my job interview, I was not only offered the opportunity to move, but I had also found the new place I would now call my own home away home.

But as thrilled as I was about this exciting chapter in my life that was about to unravel, I felt completely overwhelmed and broken down. Because the truth of it all never escaped me for one second. It was the first thing I thought of when I signed my new lease papers and didn't care when my eyes watered in front of the apartment manager, as she looked at me perplexed by my wave of emotion. And it was in the back of my mind when I drove by Old Towne and Tavern, the bar Declan and I used to go to when he asked me to be vulnerable, and hours later made me his girlfriend.

No, it wasn't supposed to be this way.

I was supposed to be sharing this joyous time with Declan, as we planned it months earlier when we sat in his backyard and talked about our dreams of me moving to Georgia, of getting our own house and starting our own family life. This was supposed to be our moment, together.

I texted Declan moments after I got the editorial job, and although he knew I would be apartment hunting that weekend, he didn't reach out. Our reality was now vastly different from the feelings of bliss I nestled into six months prior. I couldn't understand it and I couldn't make sense of it, but I finally realized there was no point in even trying. What had my dream been for so long was now only mine to live out and make of it something new. With or without him.

My last remaining days in South Florida were harder than I care to admit, even as I tried to shove any distressing thoughts I had to the side and out of my mind. When it was almost that time to go, I donated half of all my belongings to the Salvation Army and loaded everything else to the back of my Ford Escape SUV. Soon, Lumee and I would make the long drive to our home in the suburbs. But there was one thing I couldn't part with: Declan's letter to me when we broke up, from Thanksgiving. It was the one and only time he wrote me a handwritten note, and like the same pair of warm socks you wear over and over again, I still wanted it close. As if hoping that somehow those words on the paper would come to life, tied with regret and remorse, and I could still believe in his love for me.

Atlanta was still in the heavy chill of winter, so I purchased a little fleece jacket for Lumee to wear during our nine-hour drive. He wasn't used to the cold of the north, and neither was I. Then, I called up only my closest friends to say goodbye, promising my father and Oceana I would call them as soon as I turned in to my new neighborhood.

Ready or not, I knew it was time, time to embrace the bittersweet journey that awaited me. A journey of solitude and rediscovery.

On the night of my departure, I waited until it was close to midnight to leave. I wanted to start my trip in the dead silence of the night, only surrounded by my thoughts and Lumee's soft murmur as he slept. I got in my car just as the clock on my dashboard alerted me that it was now midnight. It was clear by now that almost everything in my life seemed to happen at the stroke of midnight, as if it was meant to be a sign to guide me.

The back passenger seat of my car was filled to the brim, almost over-flowing with bags of summer clothes I would clearly not be able to use for a while, along with several pairs of shoes and boxes of heavy-duty household goods. Next to me, Lumee couldn't sit still; shifting his body position every few seconds until he found a spot on his oversized bed to retrieve to for the night. So it was time. With the key in the ignition, I backed out of my park-ing space and looked behind me at the South Florida palm trees that lined my condominium one last time.

And as I began to drive past dim-lit street posts that I came to know so well, I thought back to a rainy afternoon – months before Declan came into my life again, and months before *Fireproof* became the central theme to our story.

My friend Greg was driving me home to Broward that day, after I missed catching the last city bus due to my inability to make it fast enough to the bus stop with my unreliable flip-flops on. Cruising down highway I95, we began to share stories of special people in our lives that we still held onto. The fact that "Gravity" by Sara Bareilles was playing on the radio only further encour-aged our trip down memory lane.

"Have you ever had one great love? Or have you ever experienced some-thing so magical with someone you didn't want your time together to end?" asked Greg, looking at me briefly as he continued to drive.

It didn't take a second for me to give him an answer.

"Yes, I have," I said. "I once had a very special person in my life that I met in Georgia. His name was Declan, and the connection I shared with him was beyond my wildest dreams. Everything I felt and everything I experienced with him was indescribable."

"So, what happened?"

"I dunno," I shrugged. "We had these incredible few months together then it all just came to a crashing halt. He then suddenly disappeared and I was devastated. But I never forgot about him or the chemistry we had. I guess I can venture to say he ultimately became *The One Who Got Away*."

It seemed like the radio was now on a repetitive loop to play sad love songs one after the other as we made our way down the coastal interstate, and the sound of rain beads knocked against the side of the car window. And as the rainfall came down harder with every mile, I looked outside and wondered if I could still see out into the distance.

"Do you ever think about him?" asked Greg. He was also taken by these dancing showers that continually moved like they were here to stay.

"All the time. I think about what could have been. What could have been if he had just given us a fair chance."

"I know the feeling," he sighed, offering a half-broken smile. "With great love always comes great risks, and that's the part that sucks, isn't it."

I could only nod, saddened by this simple yet difficult truth.

As it came to be, Declan did come back into my life. It took two years, many unexpected circumstances, a stroke of luck, an incredible twist of fate and a source of divine intervention to bring us together again. For a while as lovers, other times as friends, and sometimes, yes – even as distant strangers.

But what matters is that he did come back. For as long as I have known him, Declan was *"it"* for me. He was the one who showed me what it was like to believe in the magic of falling in love, and he was the one who made me reach for a love I didn't think could be mine to hold. In his presence, I was awestruck. In his presence, I was whole and exactly who I was meant to be.

Across the long stretch of highway and the endless night sky, there, off in the horizon, Georgia was waiting for me, and yet, I could see us still. I could see Declan and I laughing at his stupid *Deez Nutz* jokes, while sneaking in a kiss under the moonlight in his patio. I could see him glowing in his love for me, like the time he grabbed my face and remarked at how he had never seen such beautiful eyes.

I could still see us looking toward a future where the pain of the past no longer haunted him, because our love for each other gave us the freedom to let go. I could still see the family life we yearned for with Bella as a doting older sister to a sibling she never thought she'd have. I could still see us settling in to the hopes and dreams that found a way to manifest itself completely. And in the deep corners of my heart, I could still see God overflowing Declan and I with His everlasting love.

Because although I did not know what lay ahead once I crossed those state lines, I did know one thing: I, too, was changed. And it was all because of a man who let me rest in this sacred haven of broken beauty and captivating wonder, that over the span of several years, we came to call our own.

August 12th. 2016